Combating the Proliferation of Small Arms and Light Weapons in West Africa:

Handbook for the Training of Armed and Security Forces

Anatole Ayissi and Ibrahima Sall
Editors

UNIDIR
United Nations Institute for Disarmament Research
Geneva, Switzerland

UNITED NATIONS

NOTE

The designations employed and the presentation of the material in this publication do not imply the expression of any opinion whatsoever on the part of the Secretariat of the United Nations concerning the legal status of any country, territory, city or area, or of its authorities, or concerning the delimitation of its frontiers or boundaries.

*

* *

The views expressed in this publication are the sole responsibility of the individual authors. They do not necessarily reflect the views or opinions of the United Nations, UNIDIR, its staff members or sponsors.

UNIDIR/2005/7

UNITED NATIONS PUBLICATION
Sales No. GV.E.03.0.17
ISBN 92-9045-171-8

The United Nations Institute for Disarmament Research (UNIDIR)—an intergovernmental organization within the United Nations—conducts research on disarmament and security. UNIDIR is based in Geneva, Switzerland, the centre for bilateral and multilateral disarmament and non-proliferation negotiations, and home of the Conference on Disarmament. The Institute explores current issues pertaining to the variety of existing and future armaments, as well as global diplomacy and local entrenched tensions and conflicts. Working with researchers, diplomats, Government officials, NGOs and other institutions since 1980, UNIDIR acts as a bridge between the research community and Governments. UNIDIR's activities are funded by contributions from Governments and donors foundations. The Institute's web site can be found at URL:

http://www.unidir.org

CONTENTS

FOREWORD

This *Handbook* is a contribution to the training of the armed and security forces of West Africa. It aims to strengthen the effectiveness of these forces in the fight against the proliferation of small arms and light weapons. This initiative draws on the idea of development, peace and security for the people of West Africa enunciated by the Economic Community of West African States (ECOWAS) already in 1975.

The faith in peace, of which economic development is an essential component, impels the people of West Africa towards a future free from the scourge of armed violence. Because fundamentally human, this yearning for peace is legitimate.

Thus, the human being first. Then, the citizen. And only then, the soldier.

Beyond topics related to classical military training, the *Handbook* provides for civic education. Technical issues on the proliferation of small arms and light weapons are joined by expositions in the disciplines that contribute to the making of a good citizen: domestic law, international law, humanitarian law, human rights, international institutions, etc. The aim here is to distinguish a professional army on the one hand, from an army of mercenaries on the other, by raising the consciousness of professional soldiers and keeping them away from predatory temptation and violence.

Our armed and security forces will greatly benefit from the universal techniques and principles, as adapted for the African environment in this *Handbook*. They will find it indispensable for an effective fight against the proliferation of small arms and light weapons. They will learn about the important human qualities instilled in the professional armies of societies that value peace and security. The difficult alliance between peace and security, courage and moderation, require these qualities.

Efforts to establish peace with a view to making the future of the young West African nations safer, benefit from the support of the international community, in terms of both solidarity and friendship.

UNDP feels honored to be associated, through its regional office, with this initiative aimed at the strengthening of local West African capacities against the proliferation of light weapons. UNDP takes this opportunity to thank Belgium, Canada, Finland, France, Japan, Norway, the Netherlands, Sweden, Switzerland and the United Kingdom for their support of the activities of PCASED, notably in the implementation of the West African Moratorium on the importation, exportation and manufacture of small arms and light weapons.

Abdoulie Janneh
Regional Director
Regional Bureau for Africa
UNDP New York

PREFACE

Ten years ago, UNIDIR initiated a process of collaboration with West African states and people in the area of practical disarmament and peace building. UNIDIR's commitment aims at facilitating the establishment and strengthening of West African local capacities for the fight against the proliferation of small arms and light weapons.

The Institute, which works in partnership with civil society and political authorities, has established close collaboration with the Economic Community of West African States (ECOWAS) and the Program for Coordination and Assistance for Security and Development (PCASED). These two sub-regional institutions are in charge of development, peace and security issues in general and the fight against the proliferation of small arms and light weapons in particular.

Research is UNIDIR's main mission. Therefore, publishing and disseminating information on West African peace efforts is one of its main activities. The documents we publish aim at informing the international community on West African regional initiatives on disarmament and peace-building and appeal for stronger support for these peace efforts. These documents also archive, assess and disseminate best local practices, as well as the lessons learned from local disarmament and peacebuilding initiatives.

This joint PCASED/ECOWAS/UNIDIR publication draws its substance from West African arms control and arms regulation experiences. Written by local experts, based and working in West Africa, the *Handbook* is an essential component of efforts aiming at combating the scourge of small arms proliferation and containing violence escalation in the sub-region.

Indeed, armed and security forces have an important role to play in the fight against small arms and light weapons proliferation. For this mission to be effectively fulfilled, these forces have to be adequately trained. To this effect, the training of armed and security forces in practical disarmament measures endow them with moral values and ethical, civic and professional norms conducive to making them reliable and efficient partners that populations can depend upon.

UNIDIR, in partnership with PCASED and ECOWAS, is happy to publish this *Handbook*. Our wish is that it becomes an essential tool that will strengthen further the sense of duty and accountability amidst armed and security forces. Through this process, we hope to contribute to the edification of the broader objective of consolidation of a durable culture of peace in West Africa.

Patricia Lewis
Director
UNIDIR

THE AUTHORS

ADEJO, P. Y.
Department of State Security Service, Nigeria
ADERINWALE, Ayodele
Nigeria
AYISSI, Anatole
West Africa Programme Manager, UNIDIR
DIARRA, Cheikh Oumar (General)
Deputy Executive Secretary for Political Affairs, Defence and Security,
Economic Community of West African States (ECOWAS)
EKPANG, M. B (Ambassador)
Yacubu Gowon Center, Nigeria
FALL, Hamédine (Captain)
Chief, Operations Unit, Presidential Staff, Republic of Senegal
IREDIA, Tonnie
Director General, National Orientation Agency, Nigeria
JANNEH, Abdoulie
Regional Director, Regional Bureau for Africa, UNDP, New York
LEWIS, Patricia
Director, United Nations Institute for Disarmament Research (UNIDIR)
MULTI KAMARA, Abubakarr
Deputy Director, Programme for Coordination and Assistance for
Security and Development (PCASED)
NDIME, Djibril (Major of cavalry)
Chief, Intelligence and Communications Division, National
Gendarmerie High Command, Senegal
OCHOCHE, Sunday
Director General, Institute for Peace and Conflict Resolution, Nigeria
SALL, Ibrahima
Executive Director, Programme for Coordination and Assistance for
Security and Development (PCASED)
SALL, Alioune
Doctor of international law, lecturer (international law) and attorney
YACUBU, J. G. (Colonel)
Defense Headquarters, Ministry of Defense, Nigeria

ACRONYYMS

ANAD	Non-Aggression and Defence Assistance Agreement (Accord de non-aggression et d'assistance en matière de défense)
ECOMOG	ECOWAS Military Observer Group
ECOWAS	Economic Community of West African States
NATCOM	National Committee
OMVS	Organization for the Development of the Senegal River (Organisation pour la mise en valeur du fleuve Sénégal)
PCASED	Programme for Coordination and Assistance for Security and Development
UNIDIR	United Nations Institute for Disarmament Research
UNOPS	United Nations Office for Project Services
USSR	Union of Soviet Socialist Republics

INTRODUCTION

Boosting capacity to combat the proliferation of small arms and light weapons in West Africa: priority for local expertise

The fight against the proliferation of small arms and light weapons is a key priority on West Africa's peace and security agenda. Stopping the illegal circulation and proliferation of small arms and light weapons is such an important objective that the Economic Community of West African States (ECOWAS) Mechanism for conflict prevention, management, resolution, peacekeeping and security devotes an article (article 51) specifically to "Preventive Measures against the Illegal Circulation of Small Arms". This says that "ECOWAS shall take all the necessary measures to combat illicit trafficking and circulation of small arms".

Given that effective arms-control requires competent and responsible security forces, the Mechanism recommends such measures include "training for military, security and police forces" (article 51). "Training programmes for military, security and police forces" are stressed just as highly as a key element of the Plan of Action for the Implementation of the Programme for Coordination and Assistance for Security and Development (PCASED).

In keeping with this widely held view and the operational task that it implies, PCASED has, since its establishment, run a number of "train the trainer" courses for West African armies and security forces. This handbook is the outcome of the rewarding interactive process of building and consolidating local capacity to restore, maintain and consolidate peace.

A training handbook generally takes the form of a "cocktail" of "recipes" for action, "prepared" by "experts" for general use. It was not thought necessary to follow this classical formula in producing the present volume. Instead, PCASED has opted to spotlight the expertise of those regarded as the subregion's top experts, individuals for whom the peace and security of West Africa's peoples are a daily concern. There are two advantages to this approach. First, it is an efficient means of consolidating local capacity. Second, the end result faithfully reflects the conditions that people in West Africa confront daily.

Wherever possible we have tried to remain faithful to the original words of the authors concerned. Very slight amendments have been made here and there, chiefly for reasons of clarity. The various chapters of the Handbook, most of them produced by armed or security force officials or by civilians working with defence and security establishments, are, as one might expect, direct and forthright in tone, making the Handbook a pragmatic volume accessible to its entire target audience. Our experience of training sessions with armed and security forces shows that the message, when thus presented, is invariably better understood and assimilated by those it is addressed to.

A number of people at UNIDIR have spared neither time nor effort to have this Handbook published as soon as possible; we are particularly grateful to Patricia Lewis and Christophe Carle, the Director and Deputy Director respectively of UNIDIR, Anita Blétry, Specialized Secretary (Publications), Steve Tulliu, Editor, and Nicolas Gérard, Programme Manager and Conference Organiser.

Our thanks go also to the United Nations Office for Project Services (UNOPS), in particular Ms Roueida Khammar of the Africa Division, for support throughout the duration of this project.

Anatole Ayissi, UNIDIR
Ibrahima Sall, PCASED

PART I

The international community, peace and human security

CHAPTER 1

THE SOVEREIGN STATE IN THE INTERNATIONAL ORDER

Alioune Sall

Before speaking of the state as a sovereign entity in the international community, we must first and foremost examine the nature of the state.

DEFINITION OF THE STATE

In order to better understand the legal definition of the state, an important observation must be made. This relates to the difference between a natural person and a juridical person.

Preliminary observation: the state is a juridical person

"Juridical person" is opposed to "natural person". A natural person is a person "in the flesh" (you, me, him). A juridical person is generally an "institution" (association, trade union, business, political party, commune, department, region, state, international organization, etc.). These are said to be persons, in the legal sense, because all these entities have rights and obligations, which are distinct from those of the individuals who make them up. Thus we can speak of the rights of a trade union or an association—the right to receive donations or to bring suit in the courts, for example. Similarly, when we consider that we have suffered injury at the hands of a commune, or as a result of a decision by a body representing a state or a company, we may bring suit against the commune, state or company as an autonomous juridical person, distinct from the individuals who lead each of them.

Juridical personality enables the entity in question to exist autonomously, and hence to have its own property, to conclude contracts and to bring suit, also on its own account, to give only a few examples.

The concept of juridical personality is useful in that it enables the entity to exist above and beyond the individuals who lead it, and in particular to outlive them. It is therefore an element of continuity and permanence. Hence we speak of the continuity of the state, meaning that the state remains the same, above and beyond the individual leaders, above and beyond the different regimes and alternation in power. Leaders come and go, the state remains. It is the concept of juridical personality which makes this possible. It also guarantees a degree of security, especially at the juridical level, for all those who, for example, are led to conclude contracts or to "deal" with the state: even if the political dramatis personae change, the contracts remain valid.

Let us now examine the legal definition of the state.

The legal definition of the state

The historical, sociological and political phenomenon known as the state is traditionally defined in law in terms of three fundamental elements: territory, population and organized political power. However, these elements are not sufficient in themselves—the state must also have an essential attribute, which is sovereignty. This enables us to distinguish the state from other entities or groups which can lay claim to the same elements. Hence we can adopt the following definition, which, while not perfect, has the merit of being fairly clear: "the State is commonly defined as a group which is composed of a territory and a population falling under an organized political power and characterized by sovereignty."[1]

Let us try to analyse these categories. We will begin with the essential attribute of sovereignty.

Sovereignty as essential attribute

Sovereignty means one of two things, depending on whether it is viewed from within the state or outside it.

---

[1] Nguyen Quoc Dinh et al., *Droit international public*, Paris: L.G.D.J., 1999, p. 405.

Within its own borders, sovereignty means that the state is the supreme authority. It takes orders from no one and reports to no one. No authority is superior to it.

Externally, that is, in its international relations, state sovereignty means not that it is superior to other states, but only that it takes orders from no other authority, state or international organization. However, two very important things must be borne in mind:

- In its relations with other states or international organizations, the state cannot claim any superiority because all states are equal under the law, even if they are unequal in terms of economic or military power, area or size of population. This is why we speak of "sovereign equality". The principle of sovereignty entails the principle of equality. If states were to claim a superiority comparable to that which they enjoy in their own territory, international relations and international cooperation would be impossible.
- The principle of sovereignty, which entails equality, thus constitutes a kind of guarantee for small or weak states, because on the juridical level they will be treated in the same way as the powerful. Of course, this does not mean that states are actually equal. What is involved is only juridical equality, which is different from actual equality, but this is important. After all, we also say that "men are born free and equal", a fundamental principle in the life of a nation, even though we know that this does not amount to real equality.

Constituent elements of the state

There are three constituent elements of the state (that is, the conditions which must be met if we are to speak of a state): a territory, a population and a government. Let us analyse each of these elements:

Territory

Territory is the space within which the state exercises its authority. This space is delimited by the border. In order to prevent border delimitation between states from giving rise to conflicts, the principle of respect for borders inherited from colonization is applied, particularly in Africa. This is to avoid disputes between African states in particular concerning territorial limits which are in any event recognized as having been improperly drawn in some cases, but which would lead to many interminable disputes if they were called into question.

Population

The people living in the territory taken as a whole constitute the population. It forms what is customarily called the nation. The nation is a population which displays a degree of cohesion, a degree of unity. Nevertheless, it should be noted that special situations exist where states are composed of several nations—we speak of multinational states, such as Russia and China, for example. From the legal viewpoint, only the population category is taken into account.

Government

The government is the authority which operates in the state. It has, among other things, an administration, which carries out its wishes.

We speak of a state governed by the rule of law when the state is subject to the law, that is, when it is obliged, inter alia, to respect civil liberties, citizens' rights. It is considered nowadays that a state governed by the rule of law must respect not only the rights set out in its Constitution or its own domestic laws, but also the rights enshrined in international instruments.

The opposite of the state governed by the rule of law is the state which, for example, denies certain rights of both physical and juridical persons and asserts absolute authority. In such a state, there are few citizens' rights or none at all. When they do exist, they can easily be violated by the government authorities and asserting them in the courts is difficult. The courts offer virtually no guarantees against such violations.

The state governed by the rule of law is also assessed in terms of the way in which its power is organized—more specifically, whether or not there is a separation of powers.

The organization of power in a democratic state: separation of powers

Separation of powers is in the first place a theory. This theory was developed in particular by a French 18th-century philosopher, Montesquieu, the author of *The Spirit of the Laws.*

Montesquieu, like many earlier writers, has one aim in devising his theory of the separation of powers: to put an end to the concentration of power in the hands of a monarch, a king whose rule is described as "absolute". To this end, Montesquieu, who proceeds from the principle that anyone who has too much power may misuse it, considers that power should be divided up in order to avoid dictatorship, that this power must be separated (hence the term "theory of the separation of powers").

He therefore distinguishes between three powers within the state:

* The power to draft and adopt laws: the legislative power;
* The power to enforce these laws, in particular through the "Administration": the executive power;
* The power to interpret and apply these laws in lawsuits between citizens: the judicial power.

The separation of powers means that the powers are independent of one another, that none of them is subordinate to the other or others.

It does not, however, mean that each of the three powers operates alone or in an isolated manner. On the contrary, if the state is to work well, these powers must cooperate. The following are examples of cooperation:

* The fact that when the Government (the executive power) has negotiated an international treaty with other states or international organizations, it needs an authorization from the parliament (the legislative power) in order to fully commit the state to the treaty.
* The fact that after the law has been adopted by the Parliament (the legislative power), the Constitutional Court or Constitutional Council (the judicial power) may intervene to determine whether the law is in conformity with the Constitution, before the President (the executive power) adopts a decree promulgating the law (a decree which records the existence of a law and gives it legal force, before it is published in the official gazette of the country).

This process, which may vary in duration, is a clear illustration of cooperation between the powers: all three play a role in the process of managing the affairs of state.

Nowadays, almost all states have adopted the principle of the separation of powers. It has become one of the characteristic features of a state governed by the rule of law, or even a democratic state. In this way, we find it in the Protocol on Democracy and Good Governance, signed in 2001 by the member states of (article 1).

According to article 33 of the Protocol, "member States recognize that the rule of law involves not only the promulgation of good laws that are in conformity with the provisions on human rights, but also a good judicial system, a good system of administration, and good management of the State apparatus ...".

The state does not exist in a vacuum, even though it is sovereign. Like any individual in a society, it needs others, it is called on to maintain relations with its peers. Just as it must respect the law where its own citizens are concerned, similarly the state must comply with international law in its external relations. International law is the law which governs relations between states.

But the state may commit itself further to respecting the law when it is a member of an international organization. In such cases, the decisions taken by the organization itself (which, as we have seen, has its own legal personality, which is distinct from that of the states that make it up) are binding on the member state. In this way, the Protocols, Decisions or Regulations adopted within the Economic Community of West African States (ECOWAS) framework, for example, are, in principle, immediately binding on all the member states. The same is true, with slight modifications, in the other international organizations.

The forum above all others where states cooperate and respect the law in their common interest is the organization which embraces almost all the states in the world: the United Nations. In itself, this organization represents the voluntary restriction of state sovereignty.

COOPERATION AMONG STATES: THE UNITED NATIONS

The United Nations was set up in 1945, at the end of the Second World War. More precisely, the Charter of the United Nations, which describes its tasks and its structure, was signed on 26 June 1945.

As its name indicates, the United Nations has a universal calling, in other words, it seeks to gather together all the states in the world. It has now almost achieved this aim, since it has 191 members (in 2003).

The United Nations is not the first organization of this type. Its predecessor was the League of Nations, set up after the First World War, in 1919. But the League of Nations was unable to prevent the Second World War, because the major Powers (notably the United States) were not members, and it had no real economic or military strength.

The United Nations sought to learn from the failure of the League of Nations. This is why it not only included the major Powers, but set aside a special forum for them: the Security Council. The United Nations has economic and military powers, and it has made use of them several times, in imposing economic sanctions on certain states (such as apartheid South Africa or Iraq) or military sanctions.

Plans must be made to study the purposes and operations of the Organization.

The principal purposes of the United Nations

The United Nations has set itself a number of objectives (Articles 1 and 2 of the Charter), which may be grouped in two major categories:

- To expand international cooperation and friendly relations among states in the economic, social, political, cultural and humanitarian fields, that is, in almost all the areas of human endeavour.
- To maintain international peace and security, through prevention of threats to the peace, and the peaceful settlement of disputes between states, that is, the solving of their differences through dialogue or by judicial means (see Article 33 of the Charter), and not by means of war.

In this way, the concept of "collective security", that of "threat to international peace and security", are fundamental concepts in the Charter. They show the degree to which the issue of security is a matter of concern to the United Nations . Consequently, there is a special chapter devoted to this, in the Charter: Chapter 7, which provides the Security Council with means to act in the circumstances identified in the chapter.

The functioning of the United Nations

Mention should be made here of the various United Nations organs, highlighting the role of the most important among them. There are six of these organs:

- The General Assembly;
- The Security Council;
- The Economic and Social Council;
- The Trusteeship Council;
- The International Court of Justice;
- The Secretariat.

The General Assembly

The General Assembly is what is known as a plenary body, that is, one in which all the members of the Organization are represented. It can discuss all the problems of interest to the United Nations, that is, almost all issues.

However, the General Assembly has no direct decision-making power. It adopts resolutions which often constitute simple recommendations. "To recommend" is just to suggest, to advise, but not to dictate or to decide. This was the wish of those who drew up the Charter, in 1945.

Each state, however powerful, has only one vote in the General Assembly. This means that this United Nations organ will be dominated by the countries of the third world, which are of course the most numerous.

The resolutions of the General Assembly thus have no binding force, but they are nevertheless useful insofar as this is the only way for the poorest countries to express their views on economic and political problems. Moreover, by repeating these positions, these countries create a kind of consensus of the international community. The resolutions of the General Assembly are therefore a reflection of the thinking of the majority of states.

The Security Council

In contrast to the General Assembly, the Security Council is an organ described as having "limited membership" insofar as it has only a few members. More precisely, it is composed of 15 members, 5 permanent and 10 non-permanent. The permanent members, sometimes called the "Big Five", are: the United States, Great Britain, France, China and Russia. These five states possess a "veto", that is, the ability to "block" permanently any action by the United Nations of which they disapprove. Opposition by a single state is enough to prevent action or even a simple decision.

The non-permanent members do not possess this privilege. They are elected for a term of two years, and the composition of this group changes regularly.

Thus we may note that the Charter legitimizes inequality: if a single powerful state so wishes, the United Nations is deadlocked.

How can such inequality be justified in a world governed by the rule of law?

In fact, the United Nations sought to learn from the failure of the League of Nations. The League had established a system of strict equality among all its members, irrespective of their economic or military strength. However, when the risk of a second world war arose, the League was powerless because not only was the United States not a member, but the other Powers (Germany, Japan, USSR) had left the organization one after the other. In addition, the need for unanimity in its decisions prevented the League from reacting rapidly. The creators of the United Nations, who are essentially the victors of the Second World War, that is, the permanent members of the Council, therefore learned from that failure. They considered that it was better to be sure of being able to act under a system that was not egalitarian than to establish total equality, which though "democratic" could give rise to paralysis or ineffectiveness.

Nowadays, however, the United Nations is criticized not for the principle of inequality between members itself, but for the fact that it still reflects the state of the world in 1945. In other words, it should take account of the "new" Powers, the new international situation, and broaden the circle of permanent members to include these Powers—Germany and Japan, for example. The African states themselves claimed a permanent seat on the Security Council for the continent as a whole, on the occasion of the fiftieth anniversary of the Charter. For the moment, these claims have not led to any result.

The Security Council's field of competence par excellence is therefore the military field. It is for the Council to react to any threat to international peace. For that purpose, it has real and direct powers. In contrast to the General Assembly, the resolutions it adopts in this context of the maintenance of international peace are binding.

In extreme cases, the Security Council may impose sanctions on a state or a "rebellion". The sanctions are political (notably a blockade, that is, agreement to refrain from economic or trade relations with a state), political (a call to break off diplomatic relations with a state) or, if all these steps are ineffective, military sanctions (war waged against a state by troops supplied by member states, but under United Nations command).

We must of course distinguish between these actions designed to punish a state and peace-keeping operations.

Such operations have become very common these days. Thus the United Nations has taken action in the Middle East (Suez, Lebanon), in Congo Kinshasa (former Zaire), in the former Yugoslavia and, more recently, in East Timor, Sierra Leone and the Democratic Republic of the Congo (among other examples).

Peace-keeping operations are the opposite of war. As their name indicates, their purpose is to maintain the peace which often follows a cease-fire. The soldiers who are present seek, by interposing themselves, to prevent a resumption of hostilities. This means that such an operation is always temporary, it cannot last for ever. While it is being carried out, a final peaceful settlement must be sought. The Blue Helmets (by reference to the United Nations colour) seek to prevent war in the field, while the diplomats or politicians must work for a durable political settlement.

In its mission to safeguard peace and international security, the United Nations Security Council may call on "regional " international organizations (Examples: African Union, Southern African Development Community, ECOWAS, North Atlantic Treaty Organisation, Organization of American States, European Union, etc.). This possibility, provided for in the Charter, is based on the idea that these regional organizations are best placed to carry out "local" missions which are limited to one region of the world. That does not of course rule out peace-keeping operations conducted by the organizations themselves. The best example is supplied in this regard by ECOWAS, whose Treaty, as revised in 1993, now contains provision for such operations.

The Economic and Social Council

The Economic and Social Council includes only a few United Nations member states (a little over 50), which are elected by the General Assembly for a term of three years.

The Economic and Social Council has a simple right to make proposals. It can encourage reflection, make "recommendations" or prompt the holding of international meetings on a variety of subjects, such as economic, social, cultural, educational and other issues. Its main links are with the General Assembly and the agencies known as "specialized" in the United Nations system.

The Trusteeship Council

The Trusteeship Council is an institution which oversees the administration of certain territories, in particular in order to bring them to independence. In view of the fact that there are now almost no non-autonomous or dependent territories, the Trusteeship Council no longer functions like the other United Nations institutions. Its activities have been suspended.

The International Court of Justice

The International Court of Justice is the principal judicial organ of the United Nations. Its role is to hear cases involving disputes between states, and only such cases. It is based not in New York (as for the General Assembly and the Security Council), but in The Hague, in the Netherlands.

Under international law, a state can be brought before a court only with its consent. This stems from the principle of sovereignty, which we have already encountered. But once it has agreed to appear, it must respect the decision of the court—even, of course, if the court finds against it. Under the United Nations Charter, each member "undertakes to comply with the decision of the International Court of Justice in any case to which it is a party".

Nor does any means of coercion exist to apply to a state when it fails to enforce a court decision. However, in such cases, the Security Council may adopt sanctions against the state.

In practice, states almost always respect the decision, because they do not wish to be seen as "outlaws" within the international community. This shows that, in international relations, between states, a law does indeed exist—sometimes breached, it is true, but most often respected.

Judicial settlement, that is, submitting an issue to a court, is a peaceful means of settling a dispute. It is therefore preferable to the use of force, which is strictly forbidden under international law and the Charter (except in such cases as self-defence). The use of judicial settlement is encouraged by international law in general, and by the United Nations in particular.

The General Secretariat

The General Secretariat of the United Nations is headed by a Secretary-General. It is an important organ which can, in particular, bring to the attention of the Security Council any situation which might constitute a threat to international peace and security. It may, if appropriate, send envoys or special representatives to the field. The Security Council, which possesses decision-making power, often defers to its judgement, as set out in reports it submits directly to the Council.

CHAPTER 2

HUMAN SECURITY IN INTERNATIONAL LAW

Alioune Sall

WHAT IS HUMAN SECURITY?

First let us examine the concept of human security, in particular as regards its meaning and its content.

The concept of *human security* in fact reveals a new way of perceiving "security" in political societies (states or international organizations). "Security" is at once the absence of danger and the feeling of a certain peace of mind. The adjective "human" reflects the extension of the concept of security to the individual.

For a long time peace was essentially considered as the *absence of war* and international security as synonymous with the absence of a military threat. Hence peace meant first and foremost that weapons were silent. If there was no armed confrontation, then peace was considered to prevail.

The United Nations itself long held to this concept of international peace and security. The system of "collective security" established by the Charter rests on the idea that threats to peace cannot be other than threats of war or armed aggression.

The introduction of the concept of "human security" marks a change, in that security, by becoming "human", also encompasses an absence of non-military dangers. This development has its origin in the observation, in particular since the 1990s, with the end of the rivalry between capitalist states and communist states, that the real danger facing the world is no longer that of a major war involving two or more national armies, as hitherto, but more localized conflicts which are limited to a single country or region. In addition, most such conflicts are not military confrontations between sovereign states, but civil wars which have ethnic or separatist causes (Rwanda, the former Yugoslavia, Kosovo, Timor, etc.). Moreover, most of the victims of such conflicts are civilians.

On 31 January 1992, the Security Council, meeting at the level of heads of state and government, defined international peace and security as follows: "International peace and security are not the result of the absence of war and military conflicts alone. Other, non-military threats originate in the instability prevailing in the economic, social, humanitarian and ecological fields."

We can therefore say that the concept of "human security" means that security is no longer perceived at the state level alone, but also involves individuals and groups within the state.

When such groups—which may be ethnic, religious or political minorities—are victims of large-scale violations of human rights, international peace and security are considered to be threatened—meeting a condition for United Nations intervention through the Security Council.

It is therefore important, if we wish to properly grasp all the aspects of this concept of human security, as well as the new structure of "international peace and security", to examine the content of these human rights whose violation on a large scale can lead the international community to act.

We must also examine what happens to these human rights in a context not of peace but of conflict. There is a discipline which deals in particular with this topic: "humanitarian law".

HUMAN RIGHTS

The protection of human rights forms part of a long tradition, which is generally traced back to the origins of the revealed religions.

Since man was "created in the image of God", displaying respect for man is considered by theologians in all religions as a means of respecting God's will, and hence a way of worshipping him.

The theory of human rights was subsequently "secularized", so to speak—in other words, an explanation for the existence of these rights was no longer sought in religion or belief in God, but in pure human reason.

More specifically, it was held that alongside the rights recognized by the state through its laws, there are rights which are "natural". These are rights which man possesses simply by virtue of being born and existing. The rights in question are termed "natural" because they are inherent in the very fact of being and being human.

So this means that the state must not violate such rights, because they exist before the state does, they predate the state and are superior to it. What the state can do is to enshrine such rights—in other words "take them up", "copy" them into its laws, but it is not the state which creates them.

This line of thought has two axes:

- It distrusts absolutely religious, theological explanations. It seeks to provide justification for the institutions of society and the state on grounds of human will alone, a kind of "social contract" willed by men.
- It distrusts the state, whose power represents a threat to human rights, to freedoms. In saying that human rights are "natural" rights, this doctrine means above all that these rights are higher and even more legitimate than the state, because they existed before the state. The political authorities must yield to them; if they violate these rights, they automatically lose their legitimacy, and then the citizens have a right to insubordination and rebellion. The state and the political authorities have one purpose: to ensure the advancement of individuals and their rights. If they deviate from this purpose, they no longer have a raison d'être.

This theory of human rights emerged around the eighteenth century in the West. It inspired the English, American and French revolutions.

It still remains dominant, since the instrument which expresses it best, the *Declaration of the Rights of Men and Citizens of 26 August 1789*, appears in the constitutions of dozens of states throughout the world. The constitutions of African states almost all embody it.

Incorporating this text into the constitution means that the text enjoys constitutional—fundamental—status, and that parliamentary laws cannot violate the rights set out in the 1789 Declaration.

Another characteristic of human rights is their *universality*. In fact we speak of "human rights", without referring to a nationality or any other specific consideration. This means that these are rights that all human beings have, whatever their origin. Indeed, if human rights can sometimes be described as "natural", if they have existed since the dawn of man, this means, logically, that they cannot be dependent on anything else. In this way, the very title of the first Declaration by the United Nations General Assembly on this issue is the "Universal Declaration of Human Rights" (1948).

Lastly, human rights have become an international issue. They have given rise to the adoption of a number of instruments, some of which are:

General instruments applying to all categories of citizens of states

- 1945: The United Nations Charter itself indicates that this international organization works to promote "human rights and fundamental freedoms" (Article 55).
- 1948: The United Nations General Assembly adopts a very important resolution, which will become known as the *Universal Declaration of Human Rights*. It is the first truly universal instrument relating to human rights.
- 1966: The same Assembly adopts two *inter-national Covenants* relating to civil and political rights, on the one hand, and to economic and social rights on the other.

Specific instruments relating to certain population categories or certain offences

- 1948: United Nations Convention against the crime of genocide.
- 1949: Convention against the traffic in persons.

- 1951: United Nations Convention on refugees, followed a year later by the establishment of the Office of the United Nations High Commissioner for Refugees.
- 1953 and 56:Two protocols to the 1926 Convention relating to the prohibition of slavery.
- 1961: United Nations Convention on stateless persons (persons who do not possess the nationality of any state).
- 1979: Convention on the Elimination of All Forms of Discrimination against Women.
- 1984: Convention against Torture.
- 1989: United Nations Convention on the rights of children.

Non-universal instruments adopted by various regional organizations

- Africa: African Charter on Human and Peoples' Rights (1981)—with the African Commission on Human and Peoples' Rights.
- Europe: European Convention on Human Rights and Fundamental Freedoms (1950)—with the European Court of Human Rights.
- America: American Convention on Human Rights (1969).

All these instruments acknowledge the rights of the persons concerned. Recently, there has been an effort on the part of the international community to ensure that these rights are respected. This has taken the form of the establishment of special courts to try certain particularly serious offences, particularly in war situations:

- The Criminal Tribunal for the Former Yugoslavia, set up by the Security Council (resolution 808 adopted on 22 February 1993);
- The Criminal Tribunal for Rwanda (resolution 955 of 8 November 1994);
- The International Criminal Court, set up by virtue of the 1998 Rome Convention, under United Nations auspices. The Statute of the Court entered into force on 1 July 2002. From that date, anyone committing any of the crimes specified in the Statute is liable to prosecution before the Court. On 11 March 2003, the elected judges of the Court were sworn in.

The establishment of the International Criminal Court constitutes a twofold step forward: persons who have committed war crimes or acts of genocide may be tried by the Court, irrespective of their official duties or status; moreover, unlike the two tribunals already mentioned, this is a *permanent* court which is intended to play a lasting role. However, the Court will consider only events which took place after its establishment.

This progress in the field of human rights should not obscure the fact that difficulties arise in ensuring respect for human rights in everyday life. In particular, there is scope for the observance of human rights to be suspended, and this scope is provided for in the international conventions themselves. In this way, it is recognized that states have the right to suspend the application of these instruments—to place human rights on hold, so to speak—when they face a threat to national security, public order, public health or morals, etc. Almost all the human rights conventions contain provision for this type of exception.

The Economic Community of West African States (ECOWAS) has not lagged behind in this area of human rights in general. It reflected major world trends in adopting both instruments and attitudes which form part of the promotion of human rights and the rule of law.

It has not only vigorously condemned political violence, as manifested in coups d'état or abuses committed against civilians, but also adopted very important instruments.

The most recent is the Protocol on Democracy and Good Governance, signed in 2001, which states had to ratify if it was to enter into force. This instrument complements the 1999 Protocol relating to the Mechanism for Conflict Prevention, Management, Resolution, Peacekeeping and Security in the specific area of "prevention of internal crises, democracy and good governance, the rule of law and human rights".

The 2001 Protocol emphasizes the need for a certain degree of convergence between the member states in constitutional and political terms. The major principles on which all states should agree are as follows:

- Separation of powers;
- Democratic elections as the sole means of acceding to power;
- An apolitical army;

- A secular state and a ban on all discrimination based on religion or ethnic origin;
- Freedom to set up political parties, and the right of political parties to demand a system of public funding;
- Freedom of association, freedom of assembly, freedom to demonstrate and freedom of the press;
- A special and proper status for former heads of state.

A key innovation introduced by the Protocol will be the possibility (once the ECOWAS instrument on the Court of Justice has been revised) of bringing before the Court, which has just been established, any human rights violation in a member state, subject to a number of conditions. This will be a premiere in Africa, and an important event in international relations, since very few organizations make provision for such a right for individuals.

HUMANITARIAN LAW

Humanitarian law is the branch of international law which deals with armed conflicts. Its purpose is to introduce a little "humanity" into war, and hence it is closely related to human rights. Humanitarian law can be said to be the application of human rights in a context of armed conflict—a minimum set of rules on which all states should agree, as humanitarian considerations know no borders.

Generally speaking, international humanitarian law can be said to be composed of *two major series of rules*:

- The Hague Conventions, which relate to the regulation of war itself; and
- The Geneva Conventions (and their Additional Protocols), which relate to the protection of persons exposed to conflict in wartime.

However, a number of important events, though they were separate from these international conferences, contributed to the development of international humanitarian law.

An example was the establishment of the International Red Cross in 1859 by two Swiss, Dunant and Moynier. Nowadays the International Red

Cross is one of the most important organizations in the field of humanitarian law. More broadly, non-governmental associations and organizations play a vital role in this field. Not only do they put humanitarian law into effect, but they monitor its application by states, which, as we shall see, have concluded humanitarian treaties and conventions. Armed conflicts are inseparable from the activities of such organizations as Médecins sans Frontières, Médecins du Monde, the International Red Cross, etc.

Other milestones in the shaping of humanitarian law were:

- 1899: First Hague Conference, followed by the conclusion of a Convention;
- 1907: Second Hague Conference, also followed by a Convention.

Thus there are two *Hague Conventions* on this subject. They deal with such topics as:

- The conditions in which wars may be declared between states;
- The definition of "military objectives" (the only objectives affected by war), the status of combatants, authorized means of combat, whether in land, sea or air war;
- The conditions attached to "armistices", "peace treaties", etc.

It is clear that the Hague Conferences and Conventions ("Hague Law") relate first and foremost to the "procedure" for war, from the beginning to the end.

What of the *Geneva Conventions* ("Geneva law")?

- 1864: Geneva Convention relative to the protection of those wounded in war. It was to be amended several times.
- 1949: Four Geneva Conventions relating to:
    - amelioration of the condition of the wounded and sick in armed forces in the field;
    - protection of civilian persons in time of war;
    - treatment of prisoners of war;
    - the condition of wounded, sick and shipwrecked persons on the high seas.

- 1977: Two Additional Protocols, rounding out various aspects of humanitarian law addressed in the Conventions already mentioned:
  - Protocol No. 1: application of the rules of humanitarian law to conflicts between states, *but also to national liberation struggles;*
  - Protocol No. 2: application of humanitarian law to *civil wars.*

Above and beyond the proliferation of instruments, it can be seen that humanitarian law has undergone an expansion, it has tended to extend ever wider. More specifically, it can be noted that starting from the 1977 Protocols, humanitarian law is no longer limited to conflicts between states, but also covers non-international conflicts, and especially civil wars.

This is extremely important. This trend has had two consequences in particular.

The first is related to the fact that the conventional definition of war has proved inadequate. The majority of conflicts are longer between two or more states, but between "camps" within a single state, which has often lost legitimate authority or universal acceptance. Instead of strong states making war, it is weakened states which experience it.

Indeed, this is why the United Nations has modified its concept of security, as has already been said. Security, peace, is no longer silence on the part of the official weapons of the state, it is also peace and stability *within states, among the people.*

This is also the purpose of the Programme for Coordination and Assistance for Security and Development (PCASED) in West Africa. A determination to combat the traffic in light weapons also falls into this context: these weapons are not really used by official armies, but by groups or individuals within states, with or without political objectives.

The second consequence involves the following reasoning: if international humanitarian law also applies to non-international conflicts, the international community is entitled to "call to account" the states which fail to respect it. Armed conflict is no longer solely a "national" matter, because the rules which apply are not national, but international rules.

Hence states are bound to apply them, since they have (almost all of them) ratified the humanitarian conventions. But even if they have not ratified them, they must nevertheless respect these conventions—as everyone agrees that important humanitarian considerations are involved. In this way it can be understood that their violation constitutes a "threat to international peace and security".

After the Hague and Geneva Conventions, further instruments were added to humanitarian law:

- 1954: Convention for the Protection of Cultural Property in the Event of Armed Conflict, concluded under the auspices of the United Nations Educational, Scientific and Cultural Organization (UNESCO);
- 1981: Signature of a Convention and three protocols on prohibitions or restrictions on the use against civilians of conventional weapons which can cause injuries;
- 1993: Paris Convention on the prohibition of chemical weapons;
- 1997: Ottawa Convention on the prohibition of anti-personnel mines.

To these should be added two other United Nations General Assembly resolutions, which relate to humanitarian assistance in emergencies: they date from 1988 and 1990.

In short, these resolutions, which were adopted at the urging of humanitarian organizations operating in the field, set out the right of the victims of disasters or wars to be given assistance, and the duty of states to facilitate access to such victims. Humanitarian associations may not, however, enter a state without the consent of the authorities of that state.

It should be noted that the question of the proliferation of light weapons in West Africa constitutes a serious threat to human security and a major challenge for humanitarian law.

In recent years, organizations such as the International Red Cross or UNDP have highlighted the devastating effects of the proliferation of small arms and light weapons, particularly where civilians are concerned.

This proliferation runs counter to the fundamental rights set out in international instruments, including:

* The right to life;
* The prohibition of cruel, inhuman or degrading treatment, as well as torture;
* The right to freedom and security.

There are reported to be at least 500 million small arms and light weapons in circulation throughout the world, according to the United Nations Secretary-General in his opening statement at the Conference on the Illicit Trade in Small Arms and Light Weapons, held in July 2001. The spread of these weapons and the fact that they are in the possession of terrorist or criminal groups are at the root of a culture of violence in the societies concerned. Efforts to combat the proliferation of these instruments of death—which are among the tasks of PCASED in West Africa—thus constitute one way of contributing to respect for humanitarian law.

PART II

The Economic Community of West African States as the institutional framework for efforts to combat the proliferation of small arms

CHAPTER 3

THE ECONOMIC COMMUNITY OF WEST AFRICAN STATES (ECOWAS) AS THE INSTITUTIONAL FRAMEWORK FOR EFFORTS TO COMBAT THE PROLIFERATION OF ARMS IN WEST AFRICA

Cheikh Oumar Diarra

INTRODUCTION: PRINCIPAL ORGANS OF ECOWAS

ECOWAS was established in 1975 in Lagos. The treaty establishing the Community was revised in 1993 to include more ambitious objectives. Today, ECOWAS has 15 members, following Mauritania's withdrawal in 1999.

The principal organs of the Community are as follows:

- The Authority of Heads of State and Government, which is responsible for "the general direction and control of the Community" and for taking "all measures to ensure its progressive development and the realization of its objectives" (Treaty of ECOWAS, art. 7);
- The Council of Ministers, which is responsible for "the functioning and development of the Community" (Treaty of ECOWAS, art. 10);
- The Community Parliament, which is responsible for "promoting integration through dialogue, consultation and consensus" (Protocol relating to the Community Parliament, signed on 6 August 1994, which entered into force on 14 March 2000);
- The Community Court of Justice, which is responsible for ensuring "the observance of the law and of the principles of equity in the interpretation and application of the provisions of the Treaty"

31

(Protocol on the Community Court of Justice, signed on 6 July 1991, which entered into force on 5 November 1996);

• The Executive Secretariat, which is basically responsible for the "execution of decisions taken by the Authority and application of the regulations of the Council" (Treaty of ECOWAS, art. 19).

ECOWAS is one of the African subregional organizations that has been most concerned with questions of peace and security. Not only has it conducted peacekeeping operations in the territory of member states (Liberia, Sierra Leone and Côte d'Ivoire), it has also produced several international instruments that reflect this concern. In addition to the Treaty and its Protocols, which set out general principles, ECOWAS has adopted a moratorium and code of conduct on the import, export and manufacture of light weapons in Africa, as well as the Programme for Coordination and Assistance for Security and Development in Africa (PCASED).

GENERAL PRINCIPLES

The Treaty

Efforts to combat insecurity in West Africa are dealt with in article 58 of the revised Treaty, entitled "Regional security", which provides as follows:

"1. Member States undertake to work to safeguard and consolidate relations conducive to the maintenance of peace, stability and security within the region.

2. In pursuit of these objectives, member States undertake to cooperate with the Community in establishing and strengthening appropriate mechanisms for the timely prevention and resolution of intra-State and inter-State conflicts, paying particular regard to the need to:

(a) Maintain periodic and regular consultations between national border administration authorities;

(b) Establish local or national joint commissions to examine any problems encountered in relations between neighbouring States;

(c) Encourage exchanges and cooperation between communities [townships] and administrative regions;

(d) Organize meetings between relevant ministries on various aspects of inter-State relations;

(e) Employ, where appropriate, [good offices,] conciliation, mediation and other methods of peaceful settlement of disputes;

(f) Establish a regional peace and security observation system and peacekeeping forces where appropriate;

(g) Provide, where necessary and at the request of member States, assistance to member States for the observation of democratic elections."

This kind of provision is a new departure for ECOWAS. Before the Treaty was revised in 1993, there was no article on subregional security: in theory, therefore, the Community could not undertake action of any sort in the military domain. This is why the intervention of the ECOWAS Military Observer Group (ECOMOG) in Liberia in 1990 was criticized by jurists as being of questionable legality.

Today, this shortcoming has been rectified by the new article 58. Security has become a Community concern, and efforts to combat the proliferation of small arms are part of this general concern. The issue is mentioned specifically in the Protocol relating to the Mechanism for Conflict Prevention, Management, Resolution, Peacekeeping and Security, signed in Lomé on 10 December 1999.

Protocol relating to the Mechanism for Conflict Prevention, Management, Resolution, Peacekeeping and Security

By establishing a mechanism for conflict prevention, management and resolution and peacekeeping and security within ECOWAS, member states aim to create and consolidate the conditions in which West Africa can react promptly to crisis situations, particularly by strengthening cooperation in the areas of "conflict prevention, early warning, peacekeeping operations, the control of cross-border crime, international terrorism and proliferation of small arms and anti-personnel mines", as well as by formulating and implementing "policies on anti-corruption, money-laundering and illegal circulation of small arms" (Protocol, art. 3).

The Authority of Heads of State and Government, as the mechanism's highest decision-making body, may take decisions on "conflict prevention, management and resolution, peacekeeping, security, humanitarian support, peace-building, control of cross-border crime [and the] proliferation of small arms" (art. 6).

The question of small arms is dealt with in particular in articles 50 and 51 of the Protocol relating to the Mechanism. Article 50, on "Control of the proliferation of small arms", provides as follows:

"While taking into account the legitimate national defence and security needs, and those of international peacekeeping operations, ECOWAS shall establish effective measures to:
 (a) Control the importation, exportation and manufacture of small arms and eradicate the illegal flow of such arms;
 (b) Register and control the movement and use of legitimate arms stocks;
 (c) Detect, collect and destroy all illicit weapons;
 (d) Encourage member States to collect and destroy all surplus weapons."

Article 51, on "Preventive measures against the illegal circulation of small arms", provides as follows:

"ECOWAS shall take all the necessary measures to combat illicit trafficking and circulation of small arms. These measures shall include:
 (a) Developing a culture of peace;
 (b) Training for military, security and police forces;
 (c) Enhancing weapons control at border posts;
 (d) Establishment of a database and regional arms register;
 (e) Collection and destruction of [surplus and] illegal weapons;
 (f) Facilitating dialogue with producers and suppliers;
 (g) Reviewing and harmonizing national legislation and administrative procedures;
 (h) Mobilizing resources."

THE SIGNIFICANCE OF EFFORTS BY ECOWAS
TO COMBAT THE PROLIFERATION OF SMALL ARMS

What significance should be attached to the efforts by ECOWAS to combat the proliferation of small arms?

Firstly, it should be pointed out that these efforts did not spring from nowhere. The member states of the Community started from the premise that to reach the organization's initial objective of economic development would require a stable and peaceful environment, which the West Africa of the 1990s certainly did not provide. Civil wars, notably in Liberia and Sierra Leone, plunged the subregion into a situation of endemic insecurity which was all the more difficult to combat because it was brought about not by regular armies but by factions or rebellious forces, that is, by groups that are difficult to control.

Two factors helped make it easier for these groups to act.

On the one hand, borders are easily crossed. In West Africa, as elsewhere in Africa, borders may be not only badly demarcated, but also easy to cross. Thus, there need only be unrest in one state for the repercussions—particularly through the influx of refugees—to be felt in other states, especially neighbouring states. Unregulated movements of people facilitate the circulation of weapons. Indeed, in the 1999 Protocol, ECOWAS draws a very clear link between cross-border crime and arms proliferation.

On the other hand, the point about these arms is precisely that they are "small". They circulate easily because they are easy to transport or hide. It is therefore not a question of regulating arms in general but only a specific category of them—those that are liable to fuel civil wars or acts of banditry.

Secondly, the fact that this is a very ambitious step by ECOWAS should be highlighted. The objective ECOWAS has set itself entails legislating in an area that is a very sensitive one for states, that of national defence, and one in which they are usually reluctant to cede authority.

It should also be borne in mind that the Protocol is not just a set of simple recommendations: it is binding on all member states that have ratified it. So it is not just a list of exhortations addressed to states parties, but a set of genuine legal obligations. The states parties themselves, as members of the Community, have accepted the obligations arising under the Protocol. ECOWAS therefore has a say in certain aspects of the defence policy of member states, which may not invoke their sovereignty if they object.

Of course, any given provision of the Treaty or Protocol may go unheeded or there may be a delay in its implementation, but this does not detract from the obligation on member states to comply with Community rules in line with their undertakings.

Thirdly, ECOWAS is endeavouring, through various institutions, to take the necessary steps to implement its policy. It is not content simply to talk about combating the proliferation of small arms; it also tries to do something about it in practical terms by seeking to impose some order on the circulation of such arms. To this end, it has adopted a number of measures that fall into two broad categories: one covers action to change mentalities and attitudes—the "culture of peace" concept—while the other covers the need to control the manufacture and acquisition of weapons in member states.

This is an important element in the action by the Community, since the weapons that it is trying to prevent from proliferating are not only in the hands of combatants but also dispersed among the civilian population in towns, neighbourhoods and homes. "Small arms" are sometimes handmade and can be found or bought openly on the market. In other words, in order to prevent their proliferation it is necessary to appeal to the civilian population—the citizens of member states, who may possess them as a matter of course, if only for self-defence or as a deterrent.

In combating the proliferation of small arms, there is of course no question of making it impossible for a citizen to possess a weapon, but it is important to make people realize that possession of a weapon is a serious matter that needs to be regulated. This realization needs to be brought home at a very early age, in primary or secondary school. Civil society will also need to become involved in various ways in raising awareness.

This is the aspect stressed most in the 1999 Protocol. Several measures are envisaged for this purpose, including limiting the number of weapons in circulation, legal supervision and centralization of data on weapons, the establishment of a database and regional arms register and the initiation of a dialogue or partnership with arms manufacturers and suppliers.

Limiting the number of weapons in circulation

According to the Protocol, there are "legitimate" weapons and "illicit" weapons. The latter category refers to those that are manufactured or acquired unlawfully and are not needed for the legitimate purposes of national defence, and that lend themselves to unregulated proliferation and illicit circulation. The same ideas apply to "surplus weapons".

In principle, illicit or surplus weapons are to be destroyed.

Legal supervision and centralization of data on weapons

Weapons need to be defined and categorized in the same way in the domestic legislation of all member states, which is not the case at the moment. This is the subject of "legislative harmonization". Harmonization means that each country's domestic legislation should have the same objectives, albeit expressed in its own words. It will then be easier to adopt measures that can be applied in all ECOWAS member states.

Establishment of a database and regional arms register

The aim here, particularly through the register, is to introduce a sort of "identity card" for weapons, by identifying them with a number in order to make them easier to trace, either when they are taken from one country to another or when they are sold or borrowed.

Obviously, ECOWAS, as a regional organization, does not currently have the material resources to control the circulation of small arms in member states. This is why, with a view to boosting the credibility of its objectives, the Protocol provides for the establishment of national commissions to implement and promote all these measures and to coordinate them with measures taken at the national level.

These commissions were established by the Authority of Heads of State and Government in a decision adopted at the same time as the Protocol. They are described as "national commissions to combat the proliferation and illicit circulation of small arms" and consist of representatives of the ministries responsible for defence, the interior, security, justice, foreign affairs and civil society. Their role is to submit to the authorities all relevant proposals for combating the proliferation of small arms, undertake awareness-raising activities, cooperate and exchange experiences with the commissions from other member states, bring their work to the attention of bilateral or multilateral institutions, help the authorities to comply with their international obligations to combat the proliferation of small arms, and so on.

Initiation of a dialogue or partnership with arms manufacturers or suppliers

The idea is to stem the flow of illicit weapons: such partnerships are not of course intended to close down the arms trade, but simply to introduce, through cooperation, a little more transparency in the sale and movement of arms. The objective that ECOWAS has set for itself presupposes both "upstream" and "downstream" intervention, from the production and delivery of arms to their final use, from the international manufacturers to local owners and users.

These, then, are the general principles set out in the Treaty of ECOWAS and in the 1999 Protocol relating to the Mechanism for Conflict Prevention, Management, Resolution, Peacekeeping and Security. Efforts to combat the proliferation of small arms are included among them, alongside the Community's other concerns. Provisions that deal exclusively with this problem, and that follow on from these two general instruments, can be found in other ECOWAS legal instruments, namely:

- The Moratorium on the Importation, Exportation and Manufacture of Light Weapons in ECOWAS member states (referred to as simply the "Moratorium"), adopted on 31 October 1998;
- The plan of action for implementation of the Programme for Coordination and Assistance for Security and Development in Africa (PCASED), adopted in 1998;
- The code of conduct for the implementation of the Moratorium, adopted on 10 December 1999.

CHAPTER 4

IMPLEMENTING THE MORATORIUM ON LIGHT WEAPONS

Abubakarr Multi Kamara

INTRODUCTION

The Declaration of a Moratorium on the Importation, Exportation and Manufacture of Light Weapons, signed on 31 October 1998 in Abuja, Nigeria, by the Economic Community of West African States (ECOWAS) member states shows their resolve to prevent violence and build peace in the subregion. The Moratorium thus responds to a wish to establish an atmosphere of trust which promotes security as a basis for lasting economic and social development.

The Programme for Coordination and Assistance for Security and Development (PCASED) was set up at the request of the ECOWAS heads of state and government to ensure the effective enforcement of the Moratorium. PCASED is the technical body responsible for support for and implementation of the Moratorium.

PROGRAMME FOR COORDINATION AND ASSISTANCE FOR SECURITY AND DEVELOPMENT

PCASED is a UNDP regional programme that aims to provide technical support to ECOWAS member states in implementing the Moratorium on Light Weapons in West Africa.

The aim of PCASED is to aid and support activities which promote the creation of an atmosphere of peace and security in the interests of lasting socio-economic development. Eradicating the uncontrolled proliferation of light weapons is a requirement for establishing these conditions.

PCASED activities are implemented through effective cooperation between the ECOWAS Executive Secretariat and United Nations institutions with expertise in security and development. This partnership allows member states to improve coordination of their efforts in the fields of security, disarmament and arms control.

A meeting of Ministers of Foreign Affairs on the practicalities of implementing PCASED, held in Bamako on 24 and 25 March 1999, adopted a Plan of Action and a draft Code of Conduct (to be submitted at the ECOWAS Heads of State and Government Summit scheduled for December 1999).

Plan of Action

The Plan of Action covers nine PCASED priority areas:

- Establishing a culture of peace;
- Training programmes for military, security and police forces;
- Enhancing weapons controls at border posts;
- Establishment of a database and regional arms register;
- Collection and destruction of surplus and unauthorized weapons;
- Review and harmonization of national legislation and administrative procedures;
- Facilitating dialogue with producer suppliers;
- Mobilizing resources for PCASED objectives and activities;
- Enlarging membership of the Moratorium.

Code of Conduct

The draft Code of Conduct for the Implementation of the Moratorium on the Importation, Exportation and Manufacture of Light Weapons was adopted by the ECOWAS heads of state at the organization's twenty-second summit, held in Lomé in December 1999. The West African leaders declared that they were "aware of the compelling need to encourage and promote actions to support the effective application of the Moratorium" and "convinced that observance of the Moratorium can best be achieved through transparency and concerted effort, and that the establishment of a Code of Conduct is required for this purpose" (Preamble).

The Code of Conduct lists the institutional structures that contribute to the effective application of the Moratorium. These include, at the national level, the member states, and at the subregional level, the ECOWAS Executive Secretariat (arts. 4 and 5). All of these institutions receive support from PCASED.

In implementing the policy for controlling the proliferation of light weapons, the Code of Conduct lists the following areas of priority:

- Information exchange;
- Harmonization of legislation and administrative measures;
- Peace operations weapons register;
- Exemptions;
- Visitor certificates recording the possession of weapons in the area covered by the Moratorium (arts. 6-10).

The operational priorities are:

- Intra- and inter-state cooperation;
- Enhancing border controls;
- Collection and destruction of surplus weapons (arts. 11-13).

The Code also attaches great importance to establishing a "dialogue with suppliers and producers" of light weapons (art. 16).

The general thrust of the Code of Conduct is to bind member states to reaffirm their commitment to the control of light weapons and the establishment of a culture of peace, to respect all aspects of the ban, and to adhere to the guidelines on the importation, exportation and manufacture of light weapons, parts and munitions.

One important clause in the Code states that in order to acquire arms and munitions member states must submit a request to the ECOWAS secretariat. To this end the secretariat works with PCASED and maintains a dialogue with arms manufacturers and suppliers—the Wassenaar Group—in order to ensure that the requirements of the Code of Conduct are followed.

National commissions for the control of the proliferation of light weapons

To ensure that the Moratorium is effectively implemented at the national level, the ECOWAS states have undertaken to set up national commissions for the control of the proliferation of light weapons. Each national commission is made up of representatives from the relevant political authorities and representatives of civil society.

PCASED ACTIVITIES

PCASED has embarked on a variety of projects, in line with the Plan of Action mentioned above.

These include:

- Contribution, in June and July 1998, to the destruction of weapons collected by the United Nations Observer Mission in Liberia and the ECOWAS Military Observer Group (ECOMOG) in Liberia during the peace process.
- A plan to convert the remains of destroyed weapons into agricultural tools.
- Organization of a peace forum in Monrovia, Liberia, in July 1999.
- Organization of an expert workshop on the practicalities of establishing a database and a regional weapons register, which took place on 23 and 24 September 1999 in Accra, Ghana.
- Organization of a workshop on the humanitarian challenge posed by the proliferation of small arms, in cooperation with the Mali Red Cross and supported by NISAT (Norwegian Initiative on Small Arms Transfers), which took place on 5 and 6 October 1999 in Bamako, Mali.
- Support for a workshop on creating a civil-society coalition in Niger, March 2000.
- Organization of a subregional workshop on developing a training programme for the armed forces and security forces.
- Participation in the destruction of light weapons in Niger, in September 2000.
- Organization of national workshops for training trainers in all member states.

- Setting up a network of national commissions and strengthening their capacity to formulate their portfolios of plans at the national level.
- Organization of a large regional public awareness campaign during the 2002 Africa Cup of Nations in Mali.
- Support for national and subregional civil-society organizations in promoting a culture of peace.
- Logistical support in the form of vehicles, communication equipment and generators, provided at border control posts in Mali.
- The initiative for a mine-free West Africa.
- Collection and destruction of weapons in various member states (Mali, Liberia, Sierra Leone, Ghana, Nigeria, Togo, Niger).
- Technical assistance for a light weapons project in Chad.

PCASED INTERVENTION PRINCIPLES

PCASED works in close cooperation or in partnership with states, United Nations specialized agencies, international, regional, subregional and non-governmental organizations, civil society and local communities. PCASED primarily intervenes at the subregional level and supports initiatives in progress in the member states that reflect the specific objectives of the Moratorium; it also supports comprehensive initiatives aimed at creating a security environment that is compatible with the requirements of lasting economic and social development.

PART III

Techniques for combating the proliferation of small arms in West Africa: legal and operational aspects

CHAPTER 5

TECHNIQUES FOR COMBATING ARMS PROLIFERATION IN WEST AFRICA: LEGAL ASPECTS

Alioune Sall

INTRODUCTION

Once the political will has been affirmed, it is necessary to determine precisely the avenues, the *techniques*, to be used in combating arms proliferation (hence the title of this part).

These efforts should be conceived on two levels:

- First, through action in respect of the law, since it is most important to change legislation. This is the legal aspect;
- Next, through practical action, since it is necessary to determine which practical arrangements will be used, for example, to collect the weapons and destroy them; how will authorized stockpiles and arsenals be managed? How will border checks or the demobilization and reintegration of fighters be organized? What role will be assigned to civil society in general, young people, women, the mass media (among others)? These are operational aspects which will be addressed after this chapter devoted exclusively to the legal aspects of the issue.

LEGAL ASPECTS

Action in respect of the law will be aimed in the first place at reducing differences between one country and another, defining a minimum set of common rules: this is the "harmonization of legislation".

Next, beyond harmonization, there will be a need for centralization, the "storage" of information on weapons in circulation, a sort of central database: this is the purpose of the Register of small arms.

Harmonization of legislation

This undertaking is essential, but it cannot be taken for granted. The problems involved in the harmonization of legislation in fact revolve around three questions:

- Why is it necessary to harmonize the different sets of domestic legislation on stockpile management, circulation and use of weapons?
- Why is it difficult to harmonize this legislation?
- How can it be harmonized?

Why harmonize?

Where the circulation of weapons is concerned, the Economic Community of West African States (ECOWAS) found itself faced with a situation it hopes to change. This is not only a de facto, but also a de jure situation. This means that the Community must tackle not only a specific state of affairs which it deplores, facts which constitute an obstacle to economic development in the subregion, but also the laws and regulations which have made this state of affairs possible.

These laws and regulations vary from one country to another; they reflect diversity among the states. Even before regulating the circulation of weapons within the subregion, therefore, it is necessary first to "go back to square one" by putting a stop to the contradictions or disparities which currently exist between the laws in the member states.

Harmonization is therefore a prerequisite. It must be the sign that henceforth the states are speaking the same language where small arms and light weapons are concerned, and that the legal terms refer to the same realities.

The prior definition of a common legal language, before any action is taken, is the very purpose of the harmonization of legislation. But however essential it is, such an undertaking is not easy.

Why is it difficult to harmonize domestic laws?

There are a number of obstacles to harmonization which stem from disparities between the member states of ECOWAS. The most important are the following:

- In the first place, it is not clear that all the states have adopted legislation relating to small arms and light weapons. Over a third of them failed to reply to an inquiry from the Programme for Coordination and Assistance for Security and Development (PCASED) as part of the preparations for the harmonization project. The lack of national legislation, or difficulties experienced by official departments—and even more by the public—in gaining access to it, constitute an initial problem.
- Even when they do exist, national laws were not adopted during the same period. In 2002, states such as Benin, Burkina Faso or Togo have laws or regulations dating from the 1990s, but others such as the Niger, Senegal or, to a lesser extent, Mali have legislation dating from the years of independence. It is fairly certain that these rules do not take sufficient account of the scourge of proliferation of small arms and light weapons, a scourge which has flared up recently as a result of the civil wars in Liberia and Sierra Leone in particular.
- The common language referred to above is by no means a reality today. states' rules and regulations often address different circumstances, and this poses a real problem. In this way, some states (Burkina Faso, Niger, Togo) draw a distinction between two categories of weapon: "sophisticated weapons" and "non-sophisticated weapons"; whereas other states take a different approach, for example, depending on whether the weapons can or cannot use modern munitions.
- Conditions for the granting of the various authorizations (to carry or trade in weapons) differ from one country to another. In general, in the English-speaking states, the system is less centralized than in the French-speaking states: in the former it is the Chief Inspector of Police or (in a Nigerian state) Police Commissioner who performs this role; in the latter, a ministerial authorization is needed (Burkina Faso, Senegal, Togo).
- Where the cross-border traffic in arms is concerned, while some states have set annual quotas for arms imports, by decision of the

Minister of the Interior (Benin, Mali, Senegal), others have made no specific stipulations on this point (Burkina Faso, Niger).

Only some states have provisions governing travellers, tourists and persons in transit (Benin, Burkina Faso, Niger). Similarly, the problem of stockpiling or storage of weapons, which is so important, is subject to regulation only in some states (in particular Benin and the Niger).

It is clear that these gaps, these legal voids, are to be regretted insofar as ECOWAS is seeking to regulate the traffic in arms among the countries of the subregion.

The divergences between the laws in the states themselves constitute an initial problem. There is a further problem, that of differences between these laws and the Code of Conduct adopted by ECOWAS.

It should first of all be mentioned that the member states of the Community have an obligation to modify their legislation to bring it into line with the Code of Conduct. On the one hand, this is a general international obligation: when a state concludes a convention which involves bringing its laws and regulations into line, it must *automatically* undertake any necessary changes.

At the same time, article 1 of the Code itself states that is binding in nature.

For these two reasons, states are obliged to respect it, but this dos not exactly happen, because differences still persist, although they should have been eliminated, as promised by the states.

As an illustration, here are two examples of conflict between national laws and the Code of Conduct:

• Some measures provided for in the Code have not been implemented in practice. The annual reports on arms orders or purchases by states, which should be communicated to the Executive Secretariat, are not yet notified in some cases. The harmonization of measures required for trans-border checks relating to small arms and light weapons has still not taken place. The collection and destruction of surplus weapons, which is also provided for in the Code of Conduct, has not been carried out in all member states. States need to change their laws, if only in order to comply with their commitments within ECOWAS.

- The approaches followed in national legislation and in ECOWAS are not quite the same: we have seen that the former are sometimes based on the distinction between "modern or sophisticated weapons" and "home-made weapons", but the method laid down in the Code of Conduct involves instead classifying weapons, in accordance with the United Nations nomenclature, as "pistols", "rifles", "automatic weapons", "carbines", "machine guns", "anti-tank, mortars, howitzers", "anti-personnel mines", ...

These are a number of difficulties, obstacles, which stand in the way of any effort to harmonize legislation relating to the proliferation of small arms and light weapons. Yet this effort may be envisaged.

How to harmonize?

Several methods may be contemplated. Broadly, there are two main possibilities, and a choice must be made between them.

First: standardization of legislation. This would mean eliminating any differences, in a radical manner, since there would be only one "model law" which all the states would adopt. The content would be the same irrespective of the country. In this way, the definition of categories of weapon, the conditions in which they could be acquired, sold or loaned, would be exactly the same in Benin, the Niger, Ghana, Nigeria or Togo, and so on.

Second: more simply, we can seek "harmonization" in the true sense of the word. This would involve merely eliminating contradictions between the different national laws, while they would continue to exist. Harmonizing is making the coexistence of different elements coherent— eliminating not the various laws themselves, but only the sources of contradictions between them.

It would seem preferable to adopt this second approach. It would have the advantage of respecting the specific characteristics of the states and their administrative structure. We have seen, for example, that the terms for the granting of permits could be special in the English-speaking or federal states; the "harmonization" approach would enable these special features to be respected.

But where substance is concerned, ECOWAS's objectives would remain ambitious. They would include:

- Stricter suppression of illegal home-made weapons. It has been observed that massacres or civil wars in the subregion are supplied by this output of home-made firearms. Yet most laws, which form part of the colonial heritage (the decree on weapons of 4 April 1925), deal with home-made weapons as being intended for domestic or professional use. Obviously, this approach is now outdated.
- Identical minimum penalties in all states.
- Standardization of conditions attached to the granting of authorizations to carry and trade in weapons. Throughout the member states, the conditions to be met would be the same, but the designation of the competent authorities would remain a matter for the states themselves, since it depends on their administrative structure. Such a measure would also involve "harmonization".

Register of small arms and light weapons

The Register of small arms and light weapons forms part of the above-mentioned concept of central recording of information on such weapons. In fact, a Register can be imagined at the national level and the subregional level.

At the national level, some laws require the maintenance of such a Register, at the level of the basic administrative unit. This is the case in Benin and Burkina Faso in particular. Thus we can see that the idea is not unknown in some of our states.

This Register, compiled and maintained at the local level, not only contains details of the identity of the weapons (registration number, date of manufacture, terms of acquisition, etc.), but also "tracks" them when they circulate (transfer following the death of the owner, sale, loan, etc.). Hence it is a sort of central file on small arms and light weapons.

This is the same idea that ECOWAS seeks to take up at the subregional level, in particular by means of the Moratorium.

A Register of weapons intended for peacekeeping operations would first be drawn up, so that, on the conclusion of these operations, the weapons would be re-inventoried and withdrawn from circulation (Code of Conduct, art. 8). The reason for this new rule is that the weapons circulating in the subregion often originate directly or indirectly in the theatres of hostilities. This would make it possible to prevent them from being "lost" or "disappearing", and then becoming dispersed throughout the subregion.

In addition, thought might be given to a subregional arms Register, which in practice would not be a hand-written document but would be digital in form, and would have the same purpose as the national registers. The aim would be to regulate the import and export of weapons, to identify them by means of a registration number, to issue an "ECOWAS certificate" to the holders of such weapons (along the lines of the "ECOWAS passport"), to regulate the transfer of these weapons, their stockpiling and storage.

CHAPTER 6

COOPERATION AMONG ARMED FORCES AND SECURITY FORCES IN COMBATING THE PROLIFERATION OF SMALL ARMS

J.G. Yacubu

INTRODUCTION

The excessive and uncontrolled accumulation of small arms has led to the emergence of groups of armed individuals operating across and beyond state borders: rebel movements, private militias, terrorists, drug traffickers, arms dealers, etc. In some cases, this proliferation of armed groups undermines the authority of the state and its ability to guarantee the safety of its citizens. Everyday experience in West Africa shows that the proliferation of small arms is a catalyst for crises and armed violence and helps to destabilize governments and states, in particular as a result of the activities of subversive movements, guerrilla campaigns, terrorism, drug trafficking, civil wars and other attacks on fundamental rights and human dignity. Consequently, it has become vital for all West African states to curb the proliferation of small arms.

With the aim of combating the proliferation of small arms and light weapons, the heads of state and government of the Economic Community of West African States (ECOWAS) declared a moratorium on the importation, exportation and manufacture of small arms and light weapons on 31 October 1998.

In enforcing the West African moratorium on small arms, the armed forces and security forces will be the key to any campaign aimed at halting the proliferation of small arms and light weapons. The way in which the armed forces and security forces organize, cooperate and conduct themselves will prompt the local people to comply with the law in general, and in particular the law on the monitoring and regulation of small arms.

In these efforts carried out by the armed forces, we shall take Nigeria as a case study, and endeavour to identify:

- The causes of the proliferation of small arms;
- The factors which encourage this proliferation;
- The activities by means of which the proliferation of small arms is expanding in Nigeria;
- The composition of the armed forces whose task it is to combat the proliferation of small arms;
- The areas of cooperation between the armed forces and the security forces;
- The responsibilities of the government in efforts to combat the proliferation of small arms and light weapons.

THE CAUSES OF THE PROLIFERATION OF SMALL ARMS IN NIGERIA

The proliferation of small arms in Nigeria has many causes. They include, among others, trafficking in, local manufacture of, and theft of weapons belonging to individuals or the authorities.

Trafficking in small arms

Nigeria has 770 kilometres of shared land border with the Republic of Benin, around 1,500 kilometres with the Republic of the Niger, 1,700 kilometres with Cameroon and 90 kilometres with Chad. Nigeria also has 850 kilometres of maritime border in the Atlantic Ocean.

It would be hard to find any state in the world capable of effectively controlling such extensive borders. Naturally, traffickers make use of these porous borders to smuggle into Nigeria such different and dangerous products as drugs and arms. The Deputy Comptroller-General of the Nigeria Customs Service attributes the growth in trafficking to staff shortages, the lack of modern surveillance equipment and a shortage of vehicles. The smuggling of arms and ammunition into Nigeria has reached disturbing levels. Sometimes these arms are imported into the country hidden in clothing, vehicles or kitchen utensils. For example, during the first week of August 1999, Nigerian customs intercepted six nationals of a West African country in a canoe in Lagos with 75,000 rounds of ammunition and bags containing rifles. Recent hauls by the customs service included 10,000 magazines in Ikeja (31 December 2001), as well as almost equally large hauls in Seme Border Station (February 2002) and at Tabido/Budo in Kwara state (March 2002). The Nigerian police also intercepted traffickers in Alabata, near Abeokuta, seizing 26,500 cartridges hidden in 106 boxes. The port of Warri in the Niger delta is also regarded as a centre for arms smuggling and illegal trading. The traffickers operate from ships lying at anchor on the high seas, using faster small boats for transfers. These figures represent only a tiny sample of the total numbers of arms and ammunition which enter Nigeria and circulate illegally.

Local arms production

In the 1970s and early 1980s, local arms production did not receive enough attention in Nigeria. Arms manufactured locally were mostly used for hunting and for traditional rites. However, the rise in the use of firearms for violent crime suggests that locally produced arms have become a sound and cheap alternative to imported weapons.

Theft of arms belonging to individuals or to the state

Many people supply criminals with weapons nowadays. Criminals also obtain the arms they use by means of theft. Between 1998 and 2000, 196 weapons were registered as "lost" by the Nigerian police. In Owerri, the customs service's armoury was broken into and a substantial quantity of arms was removed by unknown persons. Investigations into this break-in are still being carried out. Arms belonging to the military have also been registered as "stolen" or "lost". The recent killing of 19 soldiers and the theft of their weapons at Zaki Biam, a border town between [Benue] and Taraba, was a case where legally acquired arms subsequently fell into the hands of non-state actors who use them for nefarious purposes. However, it is particularly encouraging that the arms in question in this specific case were found and returned to the armed forces.

Aside from theft, there are reports of several attempts by civilians to obtain military arms and ammunition. Some reports refer to corrupt officials involved in these criminal activities.

FACTORS FAVOURABLE TO THE PROLIFERATION OF SMALL ARMS

Several factors are favourable to the proliferation of small arms in Nigeria. These factors are: the quest for easy profits, relatively mild punishments, the self-defence reflex and cultural practices.

The quest for easy profits

One of the major causes of the growth in the arms market in Nigeria is the unrestrained quest for profits. In recent years, those engaged in producing local weapons have made large profits from the very lucrative trade in traditional weapons. In price terms, in Nigeria, a double-barrelled shotgun costs between 50,000 and 65,000 nairas, a single-barrelled shotgun between 25,000 and 30,000 nairas; the price of pistols ranges between 3,000 and 7,000 nairas, depending on the model, the seller and the place of sale. A suspect arrested in September 2001 by the Plateau State police for unlawful possession of firearms admitted that two of the weapons in his possession had been purchased two years previously for 55,000 and 75,000 nairas. Bearing in mind the enormous profits recorded in arms trafficking, one may expect it to continue to be attractive. The armed forces and security forces should step up their cooperation in order to monitor local production of small arms and light weapons more effectively, and if possible halt it.

The self-defence reflex

The possession of weapons without a legal authorization is punishable by a prison term of four years or a fine of 100,000 nairas, or both. This punishment is an insufficient deterrent. Between 1990 and 1999, police records indicate that 12,000 individuals were arrested in Nigeria for unlawful possession of weapons. Of the total, only 500 were taken to court. The fact that not all arrests lead automatically to a trial encourages traffickers to continue their unlawful activities. In order to combat small arms proliferation and trafficking more effectively, the punishments imposed on offenders should be made more severe so as to have a real deterrent effect.

Rise in crime

The rise in the crime wave in Nigeria fuels demand for small arms and weapons of mass destruction. In response to the determination of the police to combat offences involving weapons more effectively, criminals acquire ever more sophisticated weapons. Consequently, the rise in crime leads to an increase in demand for increasingly powerful weapons. In order to operate more effectively, the armed forces and security forces should therefore work together.

One of the consequences of easy access to firearms in Nigeria is the proliferation of ethnic militias, such as the Odua Peoples Congress, the Bakassi Boys, the Tiv and Jukun militias, to mention only a few. Even if some of these militias were created with the best of intentions, their involvement in a variety of armed conflicts throws their credibility into question. The response of Nigerians to the excesses committed by these militias was the rapid and large-scale acquisition of weapons by citizens for their personal protection. In addition, inter-ethnic rivalries, or even issues involving succession within the same ethnic group, have often led to violent confrontations. It is important to remember that those involved in the fighting are not armed only by arms traffickers or ordinary citizens. Some influential members of society who have easy access to firearms—and who benefit from it—sustain the proliferation of arms. Consequently it is vital for the government's armed forces and security forces to cooperate in order to defeat these powerful and unscrupulous individuals, and thus put an end to the proliferation of weapons.

Cultural practices

In some parts of Nigeria, some types of weapons are used for traditional rites and ceremonies. Others form part of various costumes. While the Fulanis and certain other traditional communities in the north carry swords, sticks and arrows, the communities of traditional hunters who live in the west and east of Nigeria carry cutlasses and shotguns. Sometimes, cannons are fired during official ceremonies. Some communities use dynamite and other modern explosives on these occasions. This cultural attachment to weapons has encouraged the proliferation of firearms manufactured locally, notably in rural communities where culture and tradition still enjoy great respect. Experience shows that it will be extremely difficult for the armed forces and security forces to combat this sort of proliferation effectively.

Activities that encourage the proliferation of small arms

A number of circumstances and factors underlie the proliferation of small arms in West Africa in general, and in Nigeria in particular, especially violent crime, workers' revolts, subversion, sabotage, religious crises, ethnic conflict, social agitation, micronationalism, insurrection and terrorism.

Violent crime	When crimes go unpunished, citizens look elsewhere for their protection: private security teams, militias and unlawful acquisition of weapons.
Workers' revolts	Workers' revolts occur when workers present demands to their employers (the state or private enterprises) without obtaining a response. In Nigeria, the growing militancy among workers sometimes leads to acts of violence such as attacks on individuals and property, arson, looting, vandalism or hostage-taking.
Subversion	Subversion is connected with the unlawful activities of individuals or organizations which seek to discredit or overthrow a government. This type of unlawful activity includes the illegal acquisition of weapons in anticipation of the fall of a government and the subsequent disturbances connected with a breakdown in law and order.
Sabotage	Sabotage is a deliberate unlawful act committed by individuals or organizations with the aim of embarrassing or undermining a government and its security machinery, so as to create a general feeling of poor security in society. Acts of sabotage are mainly targeted on essential facilities and services such as public buildings or transport systems.

Religious crises	A religious crisis is a kind of social unrest caused by fundamentalists, in which people fight with wild passion. Each protagonist is potentially a target for the protagonists of the opposing religion. The members of each religion become easy to recruit as combatants. Religious crises spread rapidly, especially in areas where one religion is dominant over another. In such cases, the ethnic dimension constitutes a new trend in religious crises, tending to obscure the religious dimension and transform the confrontation into a political crisis. Religious and ethnic crises in Nigeria are increasingly deadly because of the sophisticated weapons involved. These crises encourage the population to acquire firearms unlawfully on a large scale for purposes of revenge or protection.
Conflicts between communities	Conflicts between communities stem from disputes between population groups, particularly in relation to land, inheritance or resource allocation. The heterogeneous nature of Nigerian society is the greatest threat to national integration. Conflicts between communities encourage the population to acquire small arms and light weapons unlawfully on a large scale for the purposes of defending themselves and upholding the pride of the community. It is generally acknowledged that this large-scale acquisition of firearms is encouraged and sponsored by prominent individuals or heads of clans.
Social agitation	Social agitation can take the form of protests, demonstrations or disturbances intended to display a loss of patience and trust in the state or another authority. Social agitation carried out by movements of young people or students in particular has acquired dangerous proportions, with demonstrators using unlawfully purchased firearms and resorting to other forms of violence for disruptive purposes.

Micronationalism	Micronationalism develops in a plural society where different groups are formed on an ethnic or tribal basis. National integration is jeopardized when these groups assert their ethnic or tribal interests in a militant manner. This ethnic militancy, which inevitably clashes with other forms of ethnic militancy, fosters the proliferation of firearms.
Insurrection/ter-rorism	Insurrection is rebellion against a government, while terrorism is connected with acts of violence and intimidation carried out for a specific purpose. Resistance movements which are engaged in armed insurrection create a crisis around certain problems such as religion, ethnicity, resource allocation and political opportunism. Insurrection and terrorism can occur only if the rebels and terrorists have previously taken care to acquire firearms, ammunition and explosives. These can of course only be acquired unlawfully.

COMPOSITION OF THE ARMED FORCES AND SECURITY FORCES IN NIGERIA

Section 217(2) of the Constitution of the Federal Republic of Nigeria deals with the armed forces of the Federation. They are composed of the army, the navy and the air force. The Constitution confers on these forces responsibility for guaranteeing national security, neutralizing rebel movements and, when called upon to do so by the President of the Republic, coming to the aid of the civil authorities to restore law and order.

The term "security machinery" covers all the bodies established under the law to maintain national peace and stability. These bodies draw their powers from the Constitution and other decisions of the National Assembly. The security machinery in Nigeria, other than the armed forces, includes:

- The Office of the National Security Adviser;
- The National Police;
- The Directorate of State Security Services;

- The National Intelligence Agency;
- The Defence Intelligence Agency;
- The National Customs Service;
- The Nigerian Immigration Service;
- The Prison Service.

In performing their constitutional functions, the security agencies may incorporate or coordinate the activities of other bodies such as the fire service, the Civil Defence Corps, the security corps, the Nigerian Legion and non-governmental organizations.

AREAS OF COOPERATION BETWEEN THE ARMED FORCES AND SECURITY FORCES

Cooperation among the various armed forces and security forces in combating the proliferation of small arms is necessary, particularly in order to:

- Bolster national and regional security;
- Reduce the risk of armed conflict, political violence, terrorism and violent crime;
- Combat and eliminate the illegal circulation of small arms;
- and, above all, put an end to human suffering.

In Nigeria, cooperation between the armed forces and the security forces exists in other areas, but not in the area of proliferation of small arms and light weapons. This necessary cooperation may take place within "special operations", with the following areas of cooperation:

- Intelligence;
- Coordination;
- Communication;
- Political objectives;
- Road blocks;
- Security cordons;
- Patrols;
- and, most importantly, the securing of the arms and munitions of the armed forces and security forces.

Intelligence

The armed forces and security forces cannot succeed in their efforts to combat the proliferation of small arms and light weapons without a proper intelligence network. The armed forces and security forces have a variety of intelligence networks. Coordinating the work of these networks to combat the illegal circulation of small arms could substantially reduce the proliferation of such weapons. It is known that small arms and light weapons are easy to transport, hide and transfer across state borders. They are weapons which can be acquired easily through legal and illegal networks. Only appropriate intelligence services can help in an effective way to identify the groups and individuals that are engaged in the manufacture, sale, storage, transfer, possession and illegal funding of this category of weapon. This will call for sophisticated intelligence equipment such as electronic communication facilities, scanners, digital fingerprinting machines, radios, computers and vehicles.

Where the Federal State of Nigeria is concerned, a joint intelligence centre might be set up at the federal police headquarters, with branches in the police headquarters in each of the states. The joint centre could be directly connected to the offices of the country's other armed forces and security services, the Office of the National Security Adviser and the Ministry of Cooperation and Integration in Africa. The staff of the joint centre would be composed of at least two specially trained persons from each of the country's security agencies. The government should guarantee that the joint intelligence centre will be given the equipment and training needed to enable it to address the challenge of arms proliferation successfully.

Coordination

Appropriate coordination of the efforts of the armed forces and security forces is vital to ensure success in curbing the proliferation of small arms. This coordination should be carried out from the apex to the base of the governmental and administrative machinery, and must necessarily take into account constitutional factors, the machinery and competences of government, and the size and effectiveness of the security forces. The efforts of all the security agencies will demand the establishment of a coordinating body, enjoying appropriate authority, to harmonize the activities of the various organizations. Broadly speaking, such an organization should ensure coordination of intelligence by means of joint consultation and planning.

In Nigeria, such a body should not be established at the expense of the coordinating function of the National Security Adviser. The establishment of such a specialist body is recommended because the issue of the proliferation of small arms and light weapons is a phenomenon which could ultimately threaten the very existence of the Nigerian nation.

Communication

Success in efforts to combat the proliferation of small arms will to a large extent depend on reliable means of communication. With good communications, arms can easily be intercepted at points of transit. Similarly, the confidence of traffickers would be shaken and their knowledge of the actions and movements of the security forces would be restricted. Every security agency has its own means of communication. It is obvious that, with the possible exception of public telephones, not all means of communication are standardized. For the sake of greater effectiveness, there is a need for a joint communication centre for all the armed forces and security forces. The factors to be taken into account in establishing such a joint communication network include standardization and compatibility of equipment.

Political objectives

There should be a clear political objective and a resolute government policy on efforts to combat the proliferation of small arms. This would enable the national and subregional political authorities to improve the harmonization of their involvement in the current initiatives. The members of the armed forces and security forces should clearly understand their function, role, task and competence so as to avoid misunderstandings, friction and other rivalries which can lessen the effectiveness of actions where joint operations are concerned.

Public support is a major ingredient of the success of efforts to combat the proliferation of small arms. Gaining and keeping this support from the local people will depend on popular endorsement of the government's policy and the way in which the security forces discharge their role. If the armed forces and security forces burst into the lives of the people without adequate preparation of public opinion as to the need for such an operation, this may lead to situations involving misinformation or misunderstandings that can be exploited by the criminals being sought. The possibility that this type of situation might arise should be anticipated through the provision of appropriate public information concerning the government's security policy objectives and the expected benefits for the civilian population.

Road blocks

In efforts to combat the proliferation of small arms, constant road checks must be organized with the aim of apprehending the individuals being sought and preventing trafficking in arms and ammunition. For this purpose, road blocks should be set up on the main highways, secondary roads and even footpaths. The numbers of security personnel involved in these operations will depend on the number of roads to be covered and the volume of road traffic. Experience shows that road blocks constitute one of the most effective means of combating the proliferation of small arms at the national and subregional levels.

We might mention that appropriate and adequate coordination is the key factor in ensuring the success of road blocks. Road blocks can cause travellers problems or frighten them. Consequently it is necessary to explain to the public that road blocks are essentially preventive in nature and targeted principally on the villains in society, particularly those who do not respect the law. When this explanation is given in good time, public support is always obtained.

It is regrettable that road blocks lead to abuses and are generally regarded as a way for corrupt security personnel to extort money. However, it is true that the joint efforts of the armed forces and security forces in road checks, if properly carried out, cannot but secure the desired result of reducing the proliferation of small arms—always provided that appropriate penalties are imposed on corrupt security personnel.

Security cordons and raids by the security forces

The organization of security cordons and raids by the security forces is generally a joint operation by the armed forces and the security forces. Sometimes, this is a preliminary to effective checks on arms proliferation, enabling criminals and traffickers in arms, ammunitions and explosives to be discovered and neutralized more rapidly. Raids offer an opportunity in which the security forces have an advantage over the criminals because it is they who decide when and where to intervene. The operation can supply valuable information which can be used by the intelligence services. Constant hounding [of] arms traffickers and other criminals forces the latter to move their stockpiles of arms, ammunition and explosives regularly, thus increasing the risk that their activities will be discovered by the security forces.

If an area is cordoned off and searches are organized in it, the freedom of movement of citizens is temporarily restricted. In addition, the operation is regarded as an "intrusion" into their private lives. Hence public support may easily be lost, especially if the operation is lengthy. It is important for the intelligence services to provide reliable information which can guarantee that the work of the security services will be fruitful, given the substantial risk of unpopularity which can ensue if the raid produces no results. Once it is generally known that the raid by the patrols has produced results, the innocent population which has been inconvenienced during the operation will conclude that the disruption was justified.

Patrols

Patrols constitute an important area of cooperation between the security forces in efforts to combat the proliferation of small arms. For such large states as Nigeria, patrols should be carried out not only by land, by also by air. Helicopter patrols are particularly essential because arms traffickers often avoid main roads and road blocks, so that their movements can be detected only by means of helicopter patrols.

There are two kinds of patrols which can be organized in connection with the proliferation of small arms: first, patrols carried out in cities in search of arms caches and criminals on the run, and second, patrols along state borders which are particularly extensive and sometimes inaccessible (as in the case of jungles).

Securing of arms and ammunition

An important factor in monitoring the proliferation of small arms and light weapons is the need to secure arms and ammunition belonging to the armed forces and security forces. Many legal weapons have ended up in the wrong hands because of improper storage, poor record-keeping or intrigues by corrupt security personnel. As far as the Nigerian armed forces are concerned, record-keeping for arms and ammunition is very strict. In particular, the competent authorities must be kept informed each day, week or month of the precise quantity of arms and ammunition stored in each specific place. However, even with this strict surveillance system, cases have occurred where security personnel have "lost" arms or ammunition. Consequently, it is clear that security systems with poor methods of surveillance would lead to even greater losses. Punishments for personnel from the armed forces and the security forces who cannot account for their weapons should be increased. Generally speaking, perpetrators are dismissed without the missing arms or ammunition being found. So that those who are dismissed can very easily hide the lost weapons for improper use.

Many criminals obtain their weapons through theft. Between 1998 and 2000, a total of 196 weapons were recorded as "lost" by the Nigerian police forces. In Owerri the Customs Service armoury was broken into, and a large number of weapons were removed. Cases have also been recorded where members of the armed forces, the police and other security forces have sold their weapons to criminals.

Hence there is a need to coordinate and standardize methods used to monitor and register weapons in all the security forces.

THE GOVERNMENT'S RESPONSIBILITY

The government has a heavy responsibility in monitoring the proliferation of small arms and light weapons. The prime responsibility is connected with the fact that increased circulation of illegal weapons diminishes the government's credibility, owing to its inability to curb the phenomenon and combat the major crime that inevitably results. The second responsibility relates to the issue by the government of permits to buy weapons. In fact, in a system where citizens feel properly protected by the state, there is no need for individuals to apply for permits to buy weapons for reasons of protection. Citizens who acquire weapons for sports purposes do not need to own a weapon personally. A weapons monitoring centre can be set up where interested citizens can borrow weapons for a time and return them after use.

Other responsibilities of the government include:

- The strengthening of regulations on possession of weapons;
- The acquisition of modern equipment for detection of arms and ammunition;
- The provision of all necessary equipment to the armed forces and security forces for monitoring the proliferation of small arms;
- A survey of local arms and ammunition manufacturers so as to monitor their production and sales;
- The outlawing of all traditions and cultures which encourage the display of firearms;
- Suspension of the issue of permits to buy weapons to individuals;
- Creation of public awareness of the dangers posed by the proliferation of small arms and light weapons.

CONCLUSION

The proliferation of small arms and [its] negative consequences have become major concerns underlying a number of national, regional and international initiatives. These arms come from many sources, and they include weapons acquired legally by the armed forces and security forces, which end up in the hands of criminals as a result of theft or illegal sale. One of the most disturbing factors promoting the proliferation of small arms is the role of tradition and culture, particularly in the form of the ceremonial and ritual use of such weapons. Ultimately, it is important to note that the introduction of good governance and transparency in the management of public affairs can help to eradicate the scourge of small arms proliferation.

CHAPTER 7

COOPERATION BETWEEN CIVILIANS AND THE SECURITY FORCES IN EFFORTS TO COMBAT THE PROLIFERATION OF SMALL ARMS AND LIGHT WEAPONS

Sunday Ochoche

INTRODUCTION

There is a direct relationship between the availability of small arms and light weapons and the violent conflicts that are tearing West Africa apart. As a result of easy access to small arms, the prospects of peaceful resolution of conflicts in this subregion have become more complicated.

The signature by the Economic Community of West African States (ECOWAS) of a Moratorium on Light Weapons was a major landmark in efforts to combat the proliferation of small arms and light weapons in West Africa. This Moratorium is considered to be a bold initiative in efforts to combat these weapons. The Moratorium creates a framework within which a secure environment conducive to economic and social development can be created. At the same time, the Moratorium takes due account of the legitimate defence needs of West African states.

The Moratorium encourages the signatory states:

- To put in place effective measures to monitor the import, export, transfer and manufacture of light weapons;
- To register and monitor the movement and use of lawful arms stocks;
- To detect and destroy all unlawful surplus weapons;
- To authorize exemptions only in accordance with strict criteria, as defined in the Code of Conduct for the Implementation of the Moratorium.

The West African Moratorium enjoys the support of the international community. The United Nations has repeatedly expressed encouragement in several General Assembly resolutions adopted at its fiftieth, fifty-first and fifty-second sessions. Financial assistance from the international community is channelled through the Programme for Coordination and Assistance for Security and Development (PCASED). A number of arms producers, organized within the Wassenaar Arrangement, have declared that they will respect the Moratorium and refrain from exporting weapons to West Africa as long as the Moratorium is in place.

The Moratorium, which was signed in Abuja on 31 October 1998, entered into force on 1 November 1998 for a renewable period of three years. It was renewed in 2001.

In order to update the objectives of the Moratorium, the ECOWAS Executive Secretary was requested to convene a meeting of Ministers for Foreign Affairs and experts, in cooperation with the United Nations, to specify an operational framework for the implementation of the Moratorium within the framework of PCASED. To ensure the success of the Moratorium, support from the African Union, the United Nations and the international community is imperative.

DECISION ESTABLISHING NATIONAL COMMISSIONS FOR THE CONTROL OF THE PROLIFERATION AND UNLAWFUL CIRCULATION OF LIGHT WEAPONS

When declaring a moratorium on light weapons, the ECOWAS member states realized that this decision could be effectively implemented only if it enjoyed the support not only of the Governments of West Africa but also of their peoples. They also realized that if the provisions of the Moratorium were to be effective, their implementation must be monitored by national bodies in each member state. This led to the decision to establish a national commission for the control and unlawful circulation of light weapons in each ECOWAS state.

Each national commission is composed of representatives of the government (notably from the Ministries of Defence, Internal Affairs and Security, Justice and Foreign Affairs) and of civil society (non-governmental organizations, community-based organizations, community leaders, etc.). The task of this group of people is to assist the government authorities in the design and implementation of national policies for monitoring the unlawful circulation of light weapons. Each member state determines the rules governing the operation of its national commission and operates in close cooperation with PCASED. In Nigeria, for instance, the federal Government of Nigeria set up a National Committee (NATCOM) for the implementation of the Moratorium in July 2000. The Committee is composed of 12 members. One year later, in July 2001, the NATCOM carried out its first "public operation", when it publicly destroyed a stockpile of arms and ammunition seized by the security forces. A total of 1,257 weapons valued at 50 million naira[1] were destroyed. Among the weapons destroyed were 428 rifles, 494 imported pistols and 287 locally made pistols. These unlawful weapons were seized by the security forces between 1998 and 2001. In September 2001, a request by the NATCOM for the suspension of the granting of licences to carry weapons by police representatives was accepted.

Participation by West African civil society in efforts to combat the proliferation of small arms and light weapons is important, not only because civilians are the first to fall victim to insecurity fuelled by this category of arms, but also because civilians are more and more involved in trafficking in such weapons. The inability of the state to guarantee protection of individuals and communities has led to the setting up of private security units, and this has prompted an increase in demand for weapons among civilians. At the same time, faced by dissatisfied citizens, governments can be tempted to acquire more weapons in the name of "national security" and "public order".

CIVILIAN-MILITARY COOPERATION IN EFFORTS TO COMBAT THE PROLIFERATION OF SMALL ARMS AND LIGHT WEAPONS

Cooperation between civilians and the security forces in efforts to combat the proliferation of small arms and light weapons typifies interaction

---

[1] The "naira" is the Nigerian currency and its value depends on exchange rate fluctuations. At the time of writing (March 2003), 1 naira is worth roughly euro 0.0075 and US$0.0080.

between citizens and institutions lawfully responsible for security in keeping with the rules and regulations laid down by the state. The ultimate aim of this cooperation is durable peace, security and development for all.

Armed forces and security forces are in fact crisis prevention and management institutions within the state. Consequently, military expertise and professionalism have contributed to solving the problems faced by society in time of crisis. A topical example is the effort to combat organized crime in West Africa. To a certain degree, law enforcement institutions (the police and gendarmerie) are seriously overwhelmed in their capacity to fight these scourges. Consequently, it becomes necessary to call on the armed forces as a last resort. In this way, West African governments deploy joint army-police-gendarmerie patrols in order to combat organized crime effectively in the subregion. Similarly, in serious communal crises (confrontations between ethnic or religious groups), the military has often been called on for reasons of efficiency (e.g. northern Nigeria). It is clear that in this type of confrontation—interethnic or religion-based—the weapons used by those who are fighting are essentially small arms.

Given the engagement of the military in keeping order—which is exceptional—both the armed forces and the security forces need appropriate training in order to cope better with the challenges they face. In this context, it is desirable to develop an appropriate training programme. Such a programme might include the following components:

- Modern techniques for maintaining law and order;
- Small arms collection methods;
- Tracking of drugs and cross-border crimes;
- Maintenance of weapons stockpiles;
- Post-conflict demobilization of combatants;
- Disarmament and reintegration of ex-combatants into civilian life;
- Cross-border cooperation between security forces and local communities;
- Methods of spreading the culture of peace;
- Methods and techniques for maintaining arms registers.

The role of non-governmental organizations is crucial here. Civil-society organizations can help by informing the authorities of movements of arms within their communities, supporting programmes to combat corruption and the professionalization of the security forces and the customs services, promoting awareness of sound techniques of law enforcement. These organizations can also help in creating public awareness of the need for state regulation and control of arms in the possession of citizens for the purposes of self-defence.

To achieve these objectives, support from all parties is needed. And the role of the mass media can never be overemphasized here. Article 14 of the Code of Conduct for the Implementation of the Moratorium emphasizes the need for ECOWAS, in collaboration with PCASED, to develop an information programme on the Moratorium. Contributions from other civil-society groups, such as young people, women, religious orders or traditional communities, is crucial for the effective implementation of the Moratorium in particular and small arms monitoring policies in general. This is the very theme of the "culture of peace" pursued by PCASED. The fate of the West African Moratorium on light weapons will have a marked impact on the ambitions nurtured by other African subregions to set up similar disarmament and arms control instruments. Article 17 of the above-mentioned Code of Conduct recommends the extension of the Moratorium to any other African state which might be interested in the project. The persistence of areas of tension on the continent and the endemic state of war in certain regions may indeed make it necessary to extend the Moratorium in this way to states in other subregions.

CONCLUSION

The proliferation of small arms and light weapons has many causes. It is a complex phenomenon that requires a multidimensional and multi-institutional approach. Consequently, in each West African country the ECOWAS and PCASED project demands not only cooperation between civilians and the security forces, but also, in a general way, cooperation among the various governmental and non-governmental institutions and organizations involved in monitoring the proliferation of light weapons.

CHAPTER 8

COOPERATION BETWEEN STATES TO COMBAT THE PROLIFERATION OF SMALL ARMS AND LIGHT WEAPONS

Djibril Ndime

INTRODUCTION

Africa is a continent that has been torn apart. Since independence, there has been a disturbing increase in armed conflicts. Today, African wars are essentially intra-state wars, that is to say that they take place within states, and do not involve a confrontation between different states. Whether they are ethnic, political, religious or economic, these conflicts are harmful to the continent in every respect. Several African countries have experienced an implosion which has often led to massacres on a huge scale, economic and industrial collapse and meltdown of the state machinery. The outbreak of these conflicts has in most cases meant that the societies concerned have plunged into chaos (Rwanda, Burundi, Democratic Republic of the Congo, Liberia, Sierra Leone, Guinea-Bissau, Chad, Sudan, Somalia, Angola, Central African Republic, Côte d'Ivoire, etc.).

In these deplorable circumstances, leaders and civil society in Africa felt the need to find a solution so as to halt their continent's slide. In this way the idea of a regional security policy was put forward in order to break the deadlock.

The regional security policy is a global one. It seeks to pinpoint all the aspects of security in general (military strategy, protection of the population and their property, etc.) and to assign great importance to prevention.

The proliferation of light weapons occupies pride of place. Light weapons are widely used in African conflicts, in particular owing to their "advantages": they are cheap, easy to transport and conceal, simple to maintain and easy to handle.

Success in efforts to combat the proliferation of light weapons will largely depend on political will, as displayed in particular in cooperation between states. This cooperation, which is currently at an embryonic stage, should be organized on clearly spelt-out legal foundations with a well-defined strategy for action.

FOUNDATIONS OF COOPERATION BETWEEN STATES

Cooperation between states in the field of efforts to combat the proliferation of light weapons may be multilateral or bilateral.

Multilateral cooperation

The Organization of African Unity and the African Union which succeeded it assigned a major role to the security of the continent in their Charter. Even if the instruments establishing these international organizations do not explicitly refer to the proliferation of light weapons, we may consider that the issue is taken into account because of the preponderant role these arms play in conflicts in Africa.

Where subregional security is concerned, the Economic Community of West African States (ECOWAS) has been much more pragmatic and effective than the Africa-wide organization. When established, ECOWAS had a purely economic purpose. With the civil war in Liberia (1989-1997), the organization set up a subregional security arm: ECOMOG. Subsequently, following its interventions in Liberia and Sierra Leone, ECOWAS strove to adapt its instruments to the new circumstances in the subregion. The leaders of ECOWAS, having realized that there could be no development without security, decided to establish a mechanism for conflict prevention, management, resolution, peacekeeping and security.

The preamble to the Protocol relating to the Mechanism refers to cross-border crimes and the proliferation of small arms as well as their harmful consequences for stability and development in the subregion. One of the objectives of the Mechanism is "to strengthen cooperation in the areas of conflict prevention, early warning, peacekeeping operations, the control of cross-border crime, international terrorism and proliferation of small arms and anti-personnel mines" (art. 3). Other provisions specifically deal with efforts to combat the proliferation of small arms and preventive measures against the illegal circulation of small arms: these are articles 50 and 51 of the Protocol in particular.

This resolve to cooperate led to the adoption of the Declaration of a Moratorium on Importation, Exportation and Manufacture of Light Weapons in West Africa, signed on 31 October 1998 in Abuja, Nigeria. On 10 December 1999, with the aim of streamlining the implementation of the Moratorium, the member states of ECOWAS adopted a Code of Conduct for its implementation. The Moratorium was originally adopted for a renewable period of three years, and was extended in 2001. Lastly, the Programme for Coordination and Assistance for Security and Development (PCASED) was established, with assistance from UNDP, as a forum for assistance to West African states in the efforts to combat the proliferation of light weapons.

Bilateral cooperation

In this area, we may note the meetings of joint commissions involving several West African countries, which discuss issues of cooperation for security purposes, for example. Among these is a major issue: border security, especially trans-border crime and refugee issues. For example, the various joint commissions involving Senegal and Mauritania have always focused on trans-border crime, in particular on the common border (Matam, Bakel), where security is permanently poor because of the activities of armed groups. Other initiatives are helping to promote security along common borders (Nigeria and Benin, for example).

Outside this rather formal framework, there are ad hoc actions, everyday arrangements, etc. In this way state officials help one another in their tasks in an atmosphere of good-neighbourliness. Various services are provided to neighbouring countries without recourse to diplomatic channels or established procedures. This may range from meeting requests for information to the arrest of offenders in one state and their transfer to the place where the offence was committed.

AREAS OF COOPERATION POLICY

Cooperation between states mainly takes the form of exchanges of information, joint surveillance of borders and judicial assistance.

Seeking, exchanging and making use of information

This is an extremely important aspect of cooperation between states, since information occupies pride of place in efforts to combat the proliferation of light weapons. Without reliable information, no effective action can be taken against traffickers.

Today, many West African security forces, and in particular those responsible for border checks, regularly exchange (non-confidential) information with neighbouring countries. This applies particularly to Senegal and its neighbours. These exchanges cover the persons involved in arms trafficking, the types of weapon in question and the routes followed by the perpetrators. A specific case is that of cooperation between the security forces in the administrative region of Sélibaby, in Mauritania, and those of Tambacounda region in Senegal. Generally speaking, periodic meetings are organized in one of the countries as part of these exchanges of information among the security forces of different countries. Ad hoc visits are made, either to gather information, or to provide it or request a neighbour to make use of it.

This cooperation has enabled the states to apprehend many criminals who were attacking travellers on the roads, and to seize weapons of war or home-made weapons. Cooperation between Senegal and Mali led to the arrest of criminal gangs. A marked reduction in trans-border crime was subsequently observed between Mauritania, Senegal and Mali, for example.

Beyond the borders, exchanges of information may occur officially between one state and another or through Interpol, whose subregional office is in Abidjan. This cooperation agency is a supplementary resource for national police forces in the states of West Africa, but also in Chad, Gabon and Cameroon. Interpol helps the police in exchanging information, particularly in the area of organized crime and arms trafficking, which are major concerns at the present time. At its November 1999 meeting, measures were recommended for improving the coordination of information relating to arms trafficking.

Border surveillance

In West Africa, the security services of neighbouring countries cooperate in particular in surveillance of their common borders. This cooperation is vital, since criminals ignore borders. In Senegal, for example, cooperation with the neighbouring states in this area takes the form of special contacts between the security services and their counterparts in other countries. The (Senegalese) mobile brigade in Sfreté regularly holds meetings with its counterparts in the neighbouring countries. In the near future, the same will be true of the gendarmerie squads and the military units. These periodic meetings are designed to coordinate joint actions in the border areas, particularly to combat the proliferation of light weapons and organized crime.

Cooperation in this area may extend as far as the organization of joint actions, such as patrols. This is currently done on the border between Senegal, Mauritania and Mali. Between Mauritania and Senegal in particular, joint patrols lasting three or four days are organized along the border. The police, gendarmerie and armies of the two countries take part. The patrols follow the two banks alternately. The villages are visited and the local people have a chance to voice their concerns to the security forces. With Mali, there have unfortunately been no patrols since 1999. In southern Senegal, after the cease-fire with MFDC, which was signed on 8 July 1993 and reaffirmed at the Banjul meeting on 26 January 2000, a mission to observe the cease-fire and the peace agreements was set up. Its task was to organize joint patrols (Senegal, the Gambia, Guinea-Bissau and MFDC) for border surveillance. This welcome initiative was unfortunately not implemented, for political reasons.

In keeping with this concern to strengthen cooperation between African states, in the interests of security, an organization of African gendarmeries will shortly be set up, and one of its priorities will be to combat the proliferation of light weapons. A meeting to establish this new organization will be held in the near future in Dakar.

Judicial cooperation

Here it is basically a question of gathering testimony or statements, collecting legal documents, making detained persons or other persons available to the judicial authorities of a state for the purpose of providing testimony.

The ECOWAS Convention on judicial cooperation in criminal matters contains no provision for persons to be arrested and held with a view to extradition. But in practice Senegal, for example, had been able to extradite persons responsible for or involved in murder on Senegalese soil. In this way a dangerous criminal who had committed a murder in Thiès region (in Senegal) and had taken refuge in the Gambia was arrested in Banjul (the capital of the country) in May 2000 by Senegalese police and brought back to Thiès, as a result of cooperation between the Gambia and Senegal.

It can thus be said that a good level of judicial cooperation prevails at the borders, where the security forces help one another in combating crime, including trafficking in light weapons. Here too, in addition to the exchange of information, offenders in one country are often arrested and handed over to the forces in the other country without special formalities. In this area, the personal relations established between the different authorities in charge of security matters on the border sometimes play a major role, making written rules of secondary importance. This has one advantage and one drawback. The advantage is the speed with which information is exchanged or apprehended persons transferred. The drawback is the risk that these practices may be unlawful.

OUTCOME OF COOPERATION

Here we will not provide statistics, but rather outline what has been achieved through cooperation and what difficulties have been encountered in this field.

What has been achieved through cooperation

Today there is a genuine political will to develop cooperation between states in combating poor security in West Africa. Politicians, supported by civil society, have recognized that the proliferation of light weapons can only be effectively combated through a concerted effort. This is important, because without political will and popular involvement, no initiative in this field can succeed.

The political will has been manifested in practical measures and actions on the ground, with varying degrees of success. For example, there has been closer cooperation between the security forces of countries which share a border. Such joint actions have led to the seizure of many weapons on Senegal's borders with Mali, Mauritania, the Gambia and Guinea-Bissau, and criminals have been arrested. Consequently, in some localities such as Dakar and areas such as Boundou (Tambacounda region), there has been a marked drop in the circulation of light weapons and crime involving firearms.

The achievements should not, however, conceal the difficulties standing in the way of greater cooperation between West African states in the security field.

Difficulties encountered

Many difficulties have been encountered. They are principally of two types. There are economic difficulties which prevent the states from allocating a substantial share of their budgets to border security. Ethical difficulties may also be encountered, in particular the fact that some individuals and some groups have a stake in such trafficking.

Economically, most of the countries in the subregion have been facing an economic crisis for several years, reducing the resources available to them to ensure national security and maintain law and order. At the subregional level, the states very often lack what they need to put into effect the commitments to which they have subscribed. In this way the lack of joint patrols between Mali and Senegal is the result of the two countries' limited resources—in terms of funds, infrastructure and personnel. The economic difficulties mean that security personnel sometimes have to go for months without being paid. These officials then become highly vulnerable to arms traffickers and other criminals (with scope for corruption or complicity), and it is very difficult to secure full and efficient cooperation from them in combating poor security.

One of the main weak points in the efforts of ECOWAS leaders to combat the proliferation of light weapons is connected with the fact that individuals or organized or informal groups in the subregion have a stake in arms trafficking. Hence there remains a gap between declarations of good intentions and the reality on the ground, in some cases.

CONCLUSION

Despite the difficulties and the limitations of the current policies, cooperation between West African states in combating poor security in general and the proliferation of light weapons and small arms in particular is on the right track. Political will on the part of the states of the subregion has taken the form of the establishment of machinery for cooperation in effectively combating the scourge of light weapons. On the ground, those responsible for putting this cooperation into practice, notably the armed forces and security forces, spare no effort to track down criminals and seize illegal arms which are in circulation. However, the task is a hard one, in particular because of the difficult economic environment experienced by most of the countries in the subregion, and the poor level of cooperation among them. Despite these limitations, the present momentum should be maintained by all those involved in efforts to combat arms proliferation in the subregion.

CHAPTER 9

BORDER CONTROLS AND CROSS-BORDER CRIME IN WEST AFRICA

Hamédine Fall

INTRODUCTION

This chapter examines the relations between the inadequacy of the border control system and cross-border crime in West Africa. It covers all 14 member countries of the Economic Community of West African States (ECOWAS): Benin, Burkina Faso, Cape Verde, Côte d'Ivoire, Gambia, Ghana, Guinea-Bissau, Guinea (Conakry), Liberia, Mali, Niger, Nigeria, Senegal and Sierra Leone.

INADEQUATE BORDER PROTECTION: A FACTOR CONDUCIVE TO CRIME

West African border control overall is poor or inadequate, in particular because of the lack of technical infrastructure and human resources. The dilapidation of border control points is compounded by the dispiritedness of the security services personnel. They are generally poorly paid and feel isolated or "abandoned", without proper working tools or proper protection, for example, against attacks by criminals and cross-border traffickers.

Generally speaking, West African boundaries are very tortuous. For example, some borders follow a river bank (Senegal-Mauritania) or the bottom of a valley (Senegal-Mali). The nature of the terrain has a considerable influence on the effectiveness of border controls. Open plains and plateaux, for instance, are more accessible than marshy areas or jungles (Guinea, Lower Casamance, Liberia, Côte d'Ivoire, etc.); similarly, desert and forest regions are extremely difficult to monitor, as are steep slopes. Surveillance of the Senegal-Gambia border, for example, is easier than on the border between Senegal and Guinea (Conakry), in the foothills of the Fouta Djallon massif.

West African borders are extremely long and as a result border surveillance is costly.

In addition, access to these long borders is difficult. The extreme sparseness of the road network in the subregion can be imagined from a glance at an administrative map of the West African states or a highway map. Surfaced roads are rare and seldom give access to borders. International roads are few and far between and are in a particularly deplorable state. Border regions are thus hard to reach and links between states are unreliable. Deficiencies of this type are conducive to all kinds of shady deals. Border zones are also the ideal refuge for criminals and major crime locations (trafficking in arms, drugs, precious stones, etc.).

THE MANY FACETS OF CROSS-BORDER CRIME

Cross-border crime is relatively recent in West Africa. It had its beginnings in the late 1970s with the outbreak or the conclusion of wars— either wars of conquest (the Spanish Sahara or Saguiet-el-Hamra) or wars of national liberation ("Portuguese" Guinea, 1958-1973). Disarmament did not always follow the end of these conflicts, and thus men were to be found "in the bush" carrying arms which they used to earn a livelihood in a poverty-stricken environment. The ethnic upheavals, the challenge to the sovereignty of states and the power struggles of certain factions in the aftermath of these conventional conflicts created endemic crisis zones where the destabilized state apparatus was no longer able to ensure proper control of borders. Such zones are to be found in southern Senegal or Mauritania and along the southern borders of Guinea (Conakry), on its border with Liberia and Sierra Leone. Porous borders make it easy for criminals to move around and for arms to circulate across frontiers. Such movements are moreover difficult to contain because of collusion between population groups in border regions. Generally speaking, local cross-border communities place ethnic loyalty above civic loyalty. In the circumstances, it is not easy for the state to track down criminals who can count on their "blood brothers" for assistance, complicity and a place of refuge on either side of the border. A link can thus be established between the cross-border regions of armed conflict (northern Liberia, Sierra Leone, Lower Casamance) and the areas where arms are trafficked and circulate illicitly and major crime proliferates. The phenomenon is the more acute in that the regions concerned are rich in minerals (Liberia-Guinea, Guinea-Sierra Leone) or agricultural products (cashew crops in Lower Casamance), or they are livestock zones (as formerly on the Senegal-Mauritania border) or areas where narcotic plants are grown and harvested (Lower Casamance, southern Guinea) or forest regions (Upper Casamance, forest regions of Guinea).

The miserable living and working conditions of the security forces and military personnel in the border regions are a major factor in the development of cross-border crime. This situation not only generates corruption but also encourages the agents themselves to turn to crime. Security agents can be observed hiring out their weapons to criminals to enable them to engage in lawbreaking in neighbouring countries. The booty is then shared out between the criminal and the owner of the weapon in clearly defined proportions. The criminals operate in villages and individual homes, using information furnished to them by their accomplices in the security forces and the military. In the event of "problems", these cross-border criminals generally receive "cover" and protection from a police accomplice. Unfortunately, many of the states in the subregion are incapable of paying the wages of their security personnel and are apparently unable to punish these lawless activities. What is more serious is that some of the higher-ranking members of the military or state hierarchy can increasingly be seen to be participating in these crimes.

Cross-border crime is certainly one of the major threats today to peace, stability and regional integration in West Africa. In a context in which criminals attack a particular state and find shelter or protection with its neighbour, it is difficult to imagine peaceful and harmonious relations being established between the two. It is a fact, for example, that numerous instances of aggression against Senegal in Lower Casamance have been initiated, prepared and carried out from the territory of neighbouring states. Such acts normally pose the problem of the right of pursuit. Exercising that right, however, could contribute to straining relations between two neighbouring states. In this regard, mention may also be made of the permanent state of tension on the border between Guinea, Liberia and Sierra Leone. It will also be recalled that the question of arms trafficking between Guinea-Bissau and Senegal led to civil war in the former country in 1998.

Cross-border crime generally operates through "networks". The system of networks (trafficking in drugs, gold and diamonds, arms, money laundering, etc.) brings into contact a number of individuals organized into a group, gang or ring. On a larger scale of organized crime, as in South America, these would be cartels, like the Medellin or Cali cartels in Colombia. In the West African subregion, drugs (cannabis) harvested in Lower Casamance in Senegal, for example, crosses the border into the two Guineas, some going on to southern Mali, from where certain quantities reach Burkina Faso and Côte d'Ivoire. Diamonds from Sierra Leone, Liberia and (in small quantities) Guinea reach Europe, America or Asia, either via the Gambia or via the south (Angola) or the east (Kenya). There is intensive smuggling of cashew nuts from Lower Casamance by armed groups. Perhaps the most pernicious crime involves diamonds, since the proceeds from their sale either permits the purchase of more deadly weapons which will be turned against the people living in the areas producing them or goes to enrich the exporters, thus widening the gap between rich and poor in these impoverished countries—naturally preparing the way for bloody settlements of accounts in which the state is one of the main victims.

HOW CAN BORDER CONTROLS BE IMPROVED IN COMBATING CROSS-BORDER CRIME?

Border controls and the fight against cross-border crime demand very considerable human, material and financial resources beyond the capacity of individual West African states. Inter-state cooperation is thus a necessary part of combating this form of crime efficiently. Two levels of cooperation are possible here—national and subregional.

At the national level, states must:

- Reinforce border controls through the adequate and efficient presence of customs and border security personnel; and
- Abandon in part the sacrosanct principle of national sovereignty which makes a border a sacred, intangible, inalienable and impassable boundary. Useful results can only be hoped for if

neighbouring states establish common areas for border controls, particularly in "sensitive" zones (Senegal-Guinea-Bissau, Sierra Leone-Liberia, Liberia-Guinea, Côte d'Ivoire-Burkina Faso, Mali-Niger, etc.).

At the international level, West African states must:

- Take the necessary steps to ratify existing conventions and ensure their wide circulation (ECOWAS conventions, Non-Aggression and Defence Assistance Agreement (ANAD));
- Harmonize the various state laws concerning control of border areas and penalties for customs and cross-border offences;
- Establish working committees of experts in the security field (justice, gendarmerie, customs, water and forestry, defence, local government) to identify the conditions and the fundamental principles of this harmonization policy;
- Fulfil the commitments they have entered into;
- Accede to international legal instruments to combat organized crime, in particular:

  - The 1988 United Nations Convention against Illicit Traffic in Narcotic Drugs and Psychotropic Substances;
  - The Washington Convention on International Trade in Endangered Species of Wild Fauna and Flora;
  - The 1970 UNESCO [United Nations Educational, Scientific and Cultural Organization] Convention on the Means of Prohibiting and Preventing the Illicit Import, Export and Transfer of Ownership of Cultural Property;
  - The International Convention on Mutual Administrative Assistance for the Prevention, Investigation and Repression of Customs Offences, signed in June 1977;
  - The establishment of a body to follow up the implementation of legal instruments concerning subregional inter-state organizations (ECOWAS, Organization for the Development of the Senegal River (OMVS), Gambia River Basin Development Organization, Mano River Union, etc.).

Mention should also be made of the recommendations drawn up by the First Meeting of Experts of ANAD, extended to the states members of ECOWAS, on cross-border crime, which took place in Yamoussoukro, Côte d'Ivoire from 17 to 20 March 1997, and those contained in the Praia Political Declaration issued together with the invitation from the Government of the Republic of Cape Verde to the heads of state and government of ECOWAS to discuss all aspects of drugs in a ministerial conference in Praia on 8 and 9 May 1997.

The ANAD meeting adopted a joint strategy to combat cross-border crime in the ECOWAS countries, built round:

- Closer surveillance of borders, in particular through an increase in the numbers of juxtaposed control points, with efficient technical facilities at their disposal;
- The establishment of a data bank on cross-border crime in each state in the subregion;
- The establishment of an institute for advanced studies and research on crime;
- The organization of permanent direct contacts and periodic meetings between heads of security services in the different states;
- The creation in the subregion of machinery responsible for the follow-up, central control and coordination of activities to combat cross-border crime;
- The creation of machinery of this type in each state.

The Praia Political Declaration sets out 17 points for the fight against drugs and indicates how they are to be achieved. It mentions the legislative provisions required and the appropriate operational instruments for protecting populations and states, along with the strengthening of cooperation in the war against drugs, illicit cannabis cultivation and money laundering. The Declaration invites heads of state to ratify the ECOWAS A-P1-7-92 Convention on Mutual Assistance in Criminal Matters and the ECOWAS A-P1-8-94 Convention on extradition.

CONCLUSION

Controlling West African borders effectively is an extremely difficult task, and as a result the combat against cross-border crime cannot be conducted efficiently. In a world of states lacking an effective capability to monitor their international boundaries, border zones obey a logic other than that of state legality. Border zones which are not subject to adequate surveillance are peripheral to the centre of political power, and end up by generating a world of their own with its own rules and laws. They have a tendency to turn into zones of lawlessness when there is no state presence or when it is not efficient enough, paving the way for crime and delinquency. Thanks to ease of movement under the guidance of local inhabitants of the territory, and the hideouts and places of refuge, borders become ideal terrain for criminals who can pass easily from one country to another (mercenaries and traffickers in arms and products of all kinds). Political instability, poverty, mismanagement and corruption divert the state officials responsible for border control from their tasks. As long as these scourges persist in the subregion and West African states do not understand the need to cooperate in order to exercise efficient control over border areas, cross-border crime will continue to be a major preoccupation in the subregion.

CHAPTER 10

CRIME AND THE CROSS-BORDER MOVEMENT OF WEAPONS: THE CASE OF NIGERIA

P.Y. Adejo

INTRODUCTION

This chapter examines the need for close cooperation between armed and security forces and local inhabitants in efforts to combat the cross-border proliferation of small arms and light weapons. Nigeria is taken as a case study. The following areas are analysed: the nature of Nigeria's borders, the security agencies operating in border areas, the areas of security interest that require cooperation, cases of border incursion, notably espionage activities, trafficking in arms and ammunition, drug trafficking, prostitution and armed robbery/banditry, as well as the efforts the Government is expected to make to tackle effectively the scourge of cross-border proliferation of small arms. The conclusion is made up of policy recommendations.

POOR BORDER CONTROLS, A FACTOR PROMOTING CRIME

Nigeria is a vast country covering 923,768 square kilometres, with more than 36,450 kilometres of land and maritime borders. The country shares its land borders with four countries: Benin, Cameroon, Chad and Niger.

To these extensive land borders must be added 853 kilometres of coastline.

It is clear that Nigeria's borders are too extensive to be effectively policed by the Nigerian security forces. The country's maritime borders cannot be effectively covered by the Nigerian Navy. Similarly, the combined efforts of the Army, the Police, the Customs and the Immigration

Service cannot effectively control the extensive land borders. In Borno State, for example, owing to the porous nature of the border with Cameroon, the border may be crossed at any point by various means of transport during the dry season, thus rendering all the Government's efforts to curb the activities of illegal aliens, bandits and smugglers ineffective.

In addition to the porous nature of Nigerian borders, the heterogeneous nature of the border communities is another source of problems. The 1884-1885 Berlin Conference, which led to the partitioning of Africa by the colonial Powers, did not take into account the tribes and ethnic groups living along the arbitrary boundaries. The result was the apportionment of tribes and ethnic groups to different countries, so that today it is difficult in some border areas in Africa to know who is a citizen of which country. For example, the Yoruba and Borgu ethnic groups live in both Benin and Nigeria; the Hausa, Mandara, Kanuri, Fulani and Kotoko groups live in Cameroon and Nigeria; the Kanembu and the Shuwa Arabs are found in Nigeria as well as in Chad, and the Hausa and Fulani live in the Niger as well as in Nigeria.

These trans-border communities are usually composed of kinsmen who owe allegiance to one another, sometimes at the expense of their governments. They intermarry and coexist peacefully across state borders. It is commonplace to come across members of the same family living on either side of a border. Such social circumstances are not conducive to the efficient policing of official state borders. The local communities know how to evade security checks. They are reluctant to volunteer the information the armed forces and security forces need, especially on cross-border trafficking. In fact, for these communities, such trafficking is simply an "honest" means of earning a living.

CROSS-BORDER SECURITY AGENCIES

Nigeria's borders are policed by a number of organizations. These coexist and perform a variety of functions:

- Nigeria Police
- Customs and Excise
- Immigration Service
- Port Health Authority

- Plant and Animal Quarantine
- National Drug Law Enforcement Agency
- State Security Service, etc.

Nigeria's French-speaking neighbours also have a *Gendarmerie nationale.*

It is important to emphasize that the security forces responsible for policing the borders can work effectively only if there is close cooperation among these forces and between them and the local communities. At present, such vital cooperation, though not completely lacking, is minimal.

AREAS OF CROSS-BORDER INSECURITY

There are several areas in which the security forces and local communities can effectively work together to police the borders effectively.

Border incursions

Between 1964 and 1994, over a period of 30 years, Nigeria recorded over 30 border incidents with Cameroon. From these incidents, and of course the recent Bakassi crisis, it is easy to see that there is no cross-border cooperation between Nigeria and Cameroon. Nor are relations between Nigeria and Chad any better. Before the establishment of joint patrol teams (made up of personnel from Cameroon, the Niger, Chad and Nigeria) in the early 1980s, there were cases where Chadian gendarmes harassed Nigerians living on some islands in Lake Chad. Breaking point was reached between April and June 1983, with the deployment of Nigerian troops to some islands in Lake Chad, namely Kinassara, Chongole, Chkwuaje, Tetewa, Koloram and Bumaram. In that year, the Government declared that the islands belonged to Chad and that their inhabitants should pay their taxes in Chad. Other border incidents were recorded in Owode and Ijofin.

Espionage

Espionage is defined as a clandestine activity designed to destabilize or procure information relating to the security, defence, economy, technology or simply the government of a target country. Espionage activities are in most cases a prelude to subversion or sabotage, with the objective of undermining a country's stability, defence or economy, for instance. Porous borders facilitate such activities. This threat can easily be overcome if there is cross-border cooperation between security forces and local inhabitants. For example, recent intelligence reports have associated a retired colonel from the Algerian armed forces with the Al-Qaeda terrorist group. The reports have it that the retired colonel is involved in arms trafficking in Africa and that he has spent time in at least two West African countries. Through appropriate cooperation between the security forces and the intelligence services, as well as the civilian population in the Economic Community of West African States (ECOWAS) countries, movements of this type can be detected and destabilizing activities neutralized.

Smuggling

The adverse effects of smuggling on the economy, society and political stability of a country cannot be overemphasized. Apart from depriving the country of foreign exchange, smuggling also poses a dangerous threat to national security. Weapons, ammunition, drugs, prohibited merchandise, expired medicines and so on are smuggled into several ECOWAS countries. At the same time, some products from these countries, such as petroleum, cocoa, coffee and foodstuffs, are taken out of the area illegally. The economic loss caused by these unlawful activities is huge, and there are great dangers for public health, national security, political stability and peace in the subregion.

Arms trafficking

Prohibited arms and ammunition find their way easily into Nigeria and several countries in the subregion. Most of the arms used by criminals and ethnic militias in Nigeria are smuggled into the country. For instance, there are reports that Chadian rebels maintain depots of arms and ammunition in caves in the Tibesti region on the border between Nigeria, Chad and the Niger. These arms are generally transported on camels to border towns and villages in the Niger and Nigeria. There they are sold illegally to Nigerians and other potential buyers. In this illegal trade, Chadian traffickers and rebels work hand in glove with kinsmen on the other side of the two borders, in Kingum, Betti, Zinder, Diffa, Sibdou and Kazawe in the Niger, and in Mallam Fatori, Maigatari and Nguru in Nigeria. A variety of weapons are sold: AK47s, light automatic rifles, pistols and bazookas. The prices range from 70,000 nairas[1] to 200,000 nairas. Many such weapons are used during interethnic or interreligious confrontations, not only in border areas but also within Nigeria.

Cross-border cooperation among security forces and between them and local communities would help to effectively stamp out the scourge of cross-border proliferation of weapons in the region, and hence to establish and consolidate a climate of lasting peace.

Drug trafficking

Drug trafficking is becoming a serious threat to the security of citizens and the states of West Africa. In Nigeria, real awareness of the threat posed by drugs began only in 1974, when Iyabo Olorunkoya, a Nigerian lady, was arrested in the United Kingdom in possession of a large quantity of Indian hemp. She was later tried and jailed by the British courts. Since then, drug trafficking by Nigerians has grown steadily. It has tremendously damaged the country's reputation and brought much hardship and humiliation to many innocent Nigerians travelling abroad. Generally, drug trafficking goes hand in hand with organized crime and trafficking in small arms and light weapons. Here too, porous or poorly policed borders make it easier for drugs to be brought into or taken out of Nigeria.

Prostitution

Women are generally involved in this practice. Years of economic recession in Nigeria in particular and in the countries of West Africa in general have bred gangs of traffickers in human beings who lure young girls with promises of lucrative jobs in Europe or America. These women, who are encouraged to expect high earnings, are generally smuggled out of the country, across porous borders. On arrival in Europe or America, they are forced to engage in prostitution. Generally these traffickers are the same individuals as those who supply the traffickers of drugs, arms and ammunition.

---

[1] The "naira" is the Nigerian currency and its value depends on exchange rate fluctuations. At the time of writing (March 2003), 1 naira is worth roughly euro 0.0075 and US$0.0080.

Theft of weapons and organized crime

The theft of weapons is a major source of arms proliferation and of organized crime, in Nigeria in particular and in the West African subregion in general. The bandits, taking advantage of the porosity of state borders, commit crimes, in Nigeria for example, and escape across the border to take refuge in a neighbouring country. The weapons are often stolen for use in committing crimes: theft of cars and other property. Cross-border criminal activities of this kind are creating serious problems between Nigeria and its neighbours—Benin, the Niger and Chad in particular. Cross-border cooperation between the local people and the security forces could make a major contribution to stamping out criminal activities of this kind.

GOVERNMENT EFFORTS TO ACHIEVE CROSS-BORDER COOPERATION

The Federal Government of Nigeria, together with its neighbours, has taken a number of measures to boost cross-border cooperation and enhance security at the borders. These measures include the establishment of joint commissions: Chad-Nigeria, Niger-Nigeria, Benin-Nigeria, Cameroon-Nigeria, a commission for the Lake Chad basin, and joint border patrols (Nigeria-Benin).

These cooperative efforts also aim at establishing peaceful coexistence between the security forces of the different countries operating along the shared borders. Such coexistence would guarantee the security of the states and above all the local people, who are the first victims of criminal activities in the border areas.

RECOMMENDATIONS

The following recommendations can help in building and consolidating cross-border trust and effective cooperation not only among the security forces operating in border areas, but also between these forces and the local people. The effective implementation of these measures could help a culture of peace to take root both in Nigeria and between Nigeria and its neighbours.

The Government should ensure that cross-border cooperative measures between Nigeria and the neighbouring countries are effectively applied and are not just empty gestures.

In addition to the joint security operations, the Government should encourage multilateral and bilateral cooperation and any action which can stamp out cross-border crimes.

Many local communities in border areas are unaware of what the Government expects of them in terms of the maintenance of peace, security and law and order. It is therefore desirable for a security education campaign to be mounted for these inhabitants, the security forces and the administrative authorities responsible for policing the borders. Effective communication should be established among the agencies responsible for policing the borders and the other security forces.

The Government should continue and strengthen the policy for the provision of social amenities in border areas, in the form of infrastructure such as schools, hospitals, electricity and drinking water, so as to gain the trust of the communities and secure their support for government policies.

As a means of combating the outflow of foreign currency, the Government should encourage the establishment of banks and markets at the main border control posts.

The Government should step up its efforts in relation to the issue of national identity cards to Nigerians, to make it easier to distinguish between Nigerians and non-Nigerians. The latter, and especially ECOWAS citizens, should benefit from the safeguards granted to them under the various agreements on freedom of movement and residence.

PART IV

Culture of peace

CHAPTER 11

FOR A CULTURE OF PEACE IN WEST AFRICA

M.B. Ekpang

INTRODUCTION

According to Archibald MacLeish, one of the founding fathers behind the Constitution of the United Nations Educational, Scientific and Cultural Organization (UNESCO), "peace is a process and a condition, not a static objective periodically achieved and lost. It is a condition of mutual confidence, [and] harmony of purpose", which promotes the "coordination of activities" allowing free men and women to live a decent life in which war is categorically rejected through the dynamic and deliberate creation of a social and human order among the peoples of the world "in which the incentives to war are neutralized by the human and spiritual advances created and achieved".

For a society which has experienced the trauma of war the restoration of peace is critical, in particular for the social, political and economic reconstruction of the country. Peace-building should thus include all efforts intended to identify and sustain structures which can consolidate security and stability and promote a new spirit of confidence on the part of individuals and communities. Such efforts must in particular include the strengthening of government institutions and assistance for formal and informal processes of political participation. Other tasks include:

- Rebuilding civil society;
- Reintegrating displaced persons in normal economic activity;
- Redefining the role of the armed forces and police in maintaining law and order;
- Bridging the gap between humanitarian aid and development assistance;
- Taking into account the specific needs of particularly vulnerable individuals and groups(women, children, etc.).

CONDITIONS FOR THE ESTABLISHMENT OF A CULTURE OF PEACE

The consolidation of peace depends on the ability of societies to manage successfully the transition from war to a state of peace in which civil order and national security are maintained on a sustainable basis. Another important requirement is the adoption of participatory modes of government. In fact the establishment of participatory institutions of good governance represents a fundamental basis for the institutionalization and consolidation of a culture of peace.

The establishment of a culture of peace within and between communities requires a collective effort. The government must be more sensitive to national issues such as poverty, social justice, responsibility, equity, minority rights, welfare of children and women's rights. All these questions merit particular attention. Government must focus its activities on mobilization and development. In this connection there is an urgent need to promote national philosophies and regional strategies for the guidance of political endeavours and economic development initiatives. The West African states must consider the construction and consolidation of a socio-political environment conducive to sustainable peace as a challenge of the first order. The conduct of leaders and state policies must not generate suspicion, fear or a feeling of discrimination or exclusion. History shows that when an environment propitious to peace is established, individuals and communities react positively, and security and stability are thus guaranteed. The key to success lies in giving each individual, without consideration of sex, class, religion or ethnicity, a stake to defend in the system and in society.

To a certain extent a culture of peace is synonymous with a culture for life. UNESCO defines the culture of peace as the set of values, attitudes, forms of behaviour and lifestyles and activities that reflects and is inspired by respect for the life of human beings and their dignity and rights, rejection of violence, and dedication to the principles of freedom, justice, solidarity, tolerance and understanding within peoples and between groups and individuals.

A genuine culture of peace can only take root within and between communities if efforts are made to construct new platforms and new networks of relationships that promote and strengthen interaction, sharing, dialogue, mutual support and collective commitment in response to the challenge of conflict. In addition, it is necessary to construct an environment of justice and social harmony such as to consolidate mutual trust between individuals and community. That implies profound consideration of the causes of intercommunity and other conflict (ethnic, religious, etc.), and a constructive quest for solutions that will help to discourage the use of violence as an alternative to the peaceful settlement of conflicts.

ETHNICITY, EXCLUSION AND PEACE DEFICIT

Ethnicity is perceived as a major cause of conflict in Africa. It is important, however, to note that membership of an ethnic group is not in itself negative. In reality, the wealth of ethnic diversity is to be celebrated. Rather, it is the negative politicization of ethnicity that generates all kinds of contradiction and violence in pluralistic societies. When combined with the decline of the state, mediocre leadership, economic deprivation, lack of education and absence of constitutional guarantees, ethnicity becomes a powerful weapon in the hands of ethnic manipulators and other warlords. As governments are unable to ensure that the needs of their population will be met in terms of food, housing, employment, social security and health, individuals have been compelled to rely on their ethnic group for assistance and protection. Most African states have no social security system. A new arrival in a big city finds no formal assistance mechanism. Someone losing their job has no support. Someone falling ill has practically no public assistance. In reality, in the daily struggle for survival, the individual has little in the way of support.

Fortunately, in this atmosphere of despair, the ethnic group is always there to provide help. Thus, gradually, ethnic associations (as well as churches, trade unions and philanthropic organizations) stand in, more or less effectively, for government authorities and provide the individual with a kind of social security or insurance. In one sense, this is a positive development. But, unfortunately, it has been accompanied by a weakening of the credibility of the state and makes people vulnerable to manipulation and ethnic seclusion. Competition aimed at breaking this "new alliance" or "source of security" generates confrontation between groups and states. Opportunist politicians quite simply exploit these divisions and frustrations and, above all, what is perceived as a lack of consideration on the part of governments concerned only with the interests of the rich. Citizens are in fact beginning to perceive these problems only from this perspective, especially if the government is dominated by one ethnic group.

The question of ethnicity poses a threat to the very existence of a number of African states. A country such as Nigeria, with at least 250 ethnic groups, suffers from great tension. Almost everywhere in Africa tremendous national tragedies have occurred owing to inter-ethnic confrontation: Rwanda, Somalia, Liberia, Congo, Côte d'Ivoire, Central African Republic, etc.

Ethnicity is a powerful force for political instability. Unfortunately, although inter-group (and inter-ethic) communication mechanisms exist in Africa, states generally pay scant attention to them, and, in some cases, deliberately combat the aspirations of certain ethnic groups or seek to impose on society by force the values of the politically powerful class. As a result, ethnic groups whose interests are not represented by the dominant elite mobilize, seek to engage the state and express their need to participate in the management of the state so as to better protect their rights and their autonomy. When these demands are ignored, the groups in question may then embark on civil disobedience, even violence, turning their anger against those in the (ethnic) groups who they consider to be responsible for their marginalization. The resultant ethnic intolerance, if not properly countered, destroys peace, leads to armed violence, and, ultimately, to war.

RELIGION, INTOLERANCE AND THE PEACE DEFICIT

Religion also appears as a major factor for instability in certain African countries. Christianity and Islam are the two major religions on the continent. Both religions preach peace. But certain politicians and elites seek to make use of religion to promote disorder and violence. With the politicization of religion, a country as volatile as Nigeria, for example, cannot avoid sinking into intercommunity violence, as shown by the Jos incident in September 2001. The cultural, political and ethnic composition of a number of countries is such that it is difficult to separate religion from other social domains, given that religion affects virtually every institution around which life develops, whether the Government, employment, politics, marriage, or, in some cases, even health. Thus it is asserted that some private hospitals refused to admit and care for the victims of the Jos tragedy who were not followers of a certain religion.

Nevertheless, it true that religion can be mobilized for unity, peace and social harmony. Those who govern should view religion as an instrument for peace rather than a factor for division.

A culture of peace can also be considered as promoting sustainable economic growth, equitably shared.

ECONOMIC DEPRIVATION AND PEACE DEFICIT

There is no direct link between economic decline and violence. However, individuals living in poverty are more vulnerable to manipulation. In a context of acute poverty, theft and violent crime involving the use of weapons proliferate, as do light and small-calibre weapons. From this standpoint it may be asserted that the economic well-being of a nation, the allocation of national resources and the degree of poverty may lead to conflict and instability. A country which is a victim of crisis, riddled with corruption, inefficient government and an incompetent elite offers fertile ground for armed violence.

The United Nations Declaration on the Preparation of Societies for Life in Peace defined, in a general sense, "peace among nations" as "mankind's paramount value, held in the highest esteem by all principal political, social and religious movements" (General Assembly resolution 33/73, of 15 December 1978).

Peace cannot be imposed on a society or a community. It must be developed from the base up. Populations and civil society are essential ingredients in this growth of peace. For the institutionalization of an enduring culture of peace to occur, every dimension of peace—economic well-being, social justice, ecological balance and curtailment of violence—must be reflected.

LAW AND CULTURE OF PEACE

Directly linked to the imperative of a culture of peace is its legal incorporation in the constitution. The constitution is a social contract binding the citizenry as a community. While the colonists left Africa with illegitimate, but legal, constitutions, the advent of military regimes on the continent swept away the constitutional tradition. Military governments obliterated the rights of citizens and demolished institutions and democratic values. In other words, militarism destroyed the institutions of peace and established a culture of violence, repression and intolerance. For a culture of peace to again take root in African communities, it is essential to secure the conclusion of a new democratic compact between the people and their governors. The enactment of a constitution is an occasion for national mobilization, public education, identification and management of the major challenges confronting the community of citizens; it also involves collective discussion of national issues. When individuals and communities are directly engaged in this process of collective discussion they understand, adopt and vigorously defend the constitution. Indirectly the culture of peace, by means of respect for the constitution, will prosper.

CIVIC EDUCATION AND CULTURE OF PEACE

The establishment of a culture of peace presupposes a well-educated people. There is a need among African peoples for reorientation, particularly among the young and in grass-roots communities, in terms of violence as a means of conflict resolution. It is the ordinary citizen who suffers most from the pain and suffering of armed conflicts. People must be educated in dialogue and tolerance.

This task may be accomplished by new mass movements establishing alternative political forums within communities.

In our efforts to construct a genuine culture of peace in West Africa, special attention should be paid to children and young people. A study by the American Psychological Association shows that when particularly exposed to violence, "children may become less sensitive to the pain and suffering of others; they may be more fearful of the world around them; and they may be more likely to behave in aggressive or harmful ways toward others". Violence profoundly affects young minds and this study recommends that political decision makers should make specific efforts to counter the effects of violence to which children are exposed, given that violence breeds violence.

It is possible to imagine the impact on children and young people of direct and prolonged exposure to traumatic violent events (Sierra Leone, Liberia, Nigeria, Côte d'Ivoire, etc.). It is obvious that children who are victims of such experiences tend to develop a thick and insensitive shell in response to attacks on the dignity and security of others, the culture they know being synonymous with a culture of infinite and limitless violence. Educated in the school of violence, these children and young people are brought to believe that the only way of making themselves heard is through violence and use of weapons, without any consideration for dialogue and alternative options for the peaceful settlement of conflicts.

In establishing a culture of peace, particular attention must be paid to education systems. Such systems are in fact foundations on which the values that underlie peace—tolerance, dialogue, integration and democracy—are constructed. Unfortunately, today, in West Africa in particular, and on the African continent in general, education systems are in decline. Many schools and universities are not worthy of the name, so decrepit and outdated have they become (lack of libraries, teachers, laboratories and educational infrastructure in general). Yet these institutions are expected to produce tomorrow's leaders!

CONCLUSION

Time is needed to build and establish a culture of peace. Time is needed to reconstruct and rehabilitate a dislocated and traumatized society (which is what many African societies today are in fact). Africa today has serious problems. However, rather than weeping over our failures or "wallowing in" our problems, we should refocus on those opportunities that encourage success and guarantee a better future. And the future is peace (without peace, there is no future). And peace is a culture.

CHAPTER 12

CIVIL SOCIETY AND THE FIGHT AGAINST THE PROLIFERATION OF SMALL ARMS AND LIGHT WEAPONS

Ayodele Aderinwale

INTRODUCTION

The proliferation of small arms and light weapons is a great security challenge with implications for socio-economic development, human security and the stability of states. In Africa, the illicit circulation and use of small arms have made political and ethnic conflicts more violent. Consequently, efforts to combat the proliferation of small arms will have to be pursued on a number of fronts. This requires a broad range of strategies, initiatives and stakeholders, cooperation between sectors and states which transcends states, organizations and interest groups.

EFFORTS TO COMBAT SMALL ARMS: INTERNATIONAL MOBILIZATION

The first United Nations Conference on the Illicit Trade in Small Arms and Light Weapons was held in New York from 9 to 20 July 2001. This meeting reminded states of the terrible consequences of the proliferation of small arms in human terms and, through a programme of action, called on governments to take urgent measures to strengthen the monitoring and regulation of small arms and light weapons, primarily at the national level.

Prior to the United Nations Conference, many meetings and initiatives on small arms, organized both by states and by non-governmental organizations, took place in Africa. A decisive moment in this process was the signature of a Moratorium on the Importation, Exportation and Manufacture of Light Weapons in West Africa by the member states of the Economic Community of West African States (ECOWAS) in October 1998. The Moratorium is both an expression of the shared political will of West

African leaders and an innovative approach to conflict prevention and peace-building. In 2000, in a similar move, the states of the Horn of Africa and the Great Lakes region adopted a declaration—the Nairobi Declaration—and a plan of action aimed at eradicating the proliferation of small arms in that region. Unfortunately, both the West African Moratorium and the Nairobi Declaration are non-binding in the legal sense.

On 30 November and 1 December 2000 the African preparatory meeting for the above-mentioned United Nations Conference on Small Arms and Light Weapons was held in Bamako, Mali. The purpose of the meeting was to draw up an African common position for the New York Conference. In the Bamako Declaration, adopted at the end of their proceedings, the African states set out a number of measures to be taken at the national, regional and international levels to create a culture of peace, improve conflict management practices, harmonize legislation on small arms and encourage development and stability in Africa.

CIVIL SOCIETY AND EFFORTS TO COMBAT THE PROLIFERATION OF SMALL ARMS IN AFRICA

The state cannot combat small arms proliferation alone. Given the scale of the disasters caused by small arms, it is imperative for civil society to define creative strategies and appropriate measures to tackle the illicit circulation of small arms effectively. This undertaking should involve everyone—hence the need to raise public awareness of what needs to be done.

Even though it is states which play a fundamental role in the creation of armed conflicts in Africa, it is civilian populations which suffer the most from the effects of these conflicts. Consequently, it is the responsibility of civil-society organizations to call on governments to put an end not only to violence but also to human suffering, as well as the conditions that sustain this violence and this suffering. Today, West African civil-society organizations are actively involved in efforts to combat the proliferation of small arms. The Programme for Coordination and Assistance for Security and Development (PCASED), which supports ECOWAS member states in combating the scourge of small arms, underlines the important role expected of civil society and local communities in the effective implementation of the West African Moratorium on light weapons, for example. At the 1998 summit, during which the Moratorium was signed, a parallel meeting of West African non-governmental organizations was held and adopted a plan of action on light weapons. Further to these efforts, the West African Network on Small Arms (WANSA) was set up.

The role of civil society in combating small arms proliferation is now widely acknowledged. The United Nations Group of Governmental Experts on Small Arms, in its report A/54/258 of 19 August 1999, recommends that the United Nations should "facilitate appropriate cooperation with civil society, including non-governmental organizations, in activities related to small arms and light weapons, in view of the important role that civil society plays in efforts to raise awareness of and address the problems associated with such weapons" (para. 105). The same report recommends that "in deciding on the timetable for the Conference, the preparatory committee provide opportunities for presentations by representatives of civil society" (para. 135).

ROLE AND RESPONSIBILITIES OF CIVIL SOCIETY

Non-governmental organizations and the other segments of civil society are active in the efforts being made by the states of West Africa to curb the proliferation of light weapons. For instance, the churches are currently playing a prominent role. Because of their deep roots in local communities, churches are well positioned to handle the conflicts that may arise there. Church leaders enjoy the confidence and respect of their congregations, and are also well informed of their needs. Moreover, churches are well positioned to give the necessary leadership in efforts to raise awareness of the nature and extent of the threat posed by small arms.

Civil-society organizations are called on to design creative strategies to curb the supply and misuse of small arms and foster the establishment of social, economic, and political conditions which are compatible with human security. In that regard, these organizations need to address as a matter of urgency the problem of violence in West Africa in general, and the issue of the diffusion and misuse of small arms in particular. The reduction of armed violence, and especially the reduction of the use of guns, requires a reduction in the demand for such weapons. This requires a radical social, economic and political transformation. Disarmament efforts can only yield positive results if they are accompanied by the creation of jobs (for young people, who are involved in the bulk of armed violence) and social conditions and basic infrastructure within societies. Civil society must stand in solidarity with individuals and communities that are victims of armed violence. For instance, non-governmental organizations could train community leaders who could in turn build awareness of the threat posed by light weapons and facilitate public participation in the process of taking decisions and implementing policies on disarmament and the regulation of the circulation of firearms in society.

The gathering and dissemination of information is indispensable in the war against the illicit use of and trafficking in light weapons. Civil society should support research efforts aimed at promoting better understanding of the challenges to be faced: the scale of gun availability, the physical and psychological consequences of the illicit use of such weapons, etc.

AN AGENDA FOR CIVIL SOCIETY

The role of civil society in combating the proliferation of small arms can be subsumed under the following headings.

Awareness-raising policy

Civil-society organizations in general, and non-governmental organizations in particular, are more competent to raise awareness of the devastating effects of the proliferation of small arms and call for the introduction of the policies and legislation needed to combat such proliferation effectively. For that purpose, non-governmental organizations can organize awareness and information campaigns on the dangers of private possession of firearms. More specifically, non-governmental organizations and other civil-society organizations should strive to:

- Ensure respect for the principle of accountability in the security sector against the culture of impunity, where it exists;
- Contribute to the manifestation of international political will and momentum so as to effectively support efforts to combat small arms;
- Denounce and combat the political, social, and economic conditions that tend to generate greater demand for firearms;

- Work for a reduction in demand for firearms, through measures to consolidate democracy, good governance, respect for human rights and the rule of law as well as economic growth;
- Reduce the secrecy associated with decision-making on weapons, organize discussions on small arms and combat public ignorance about security matters in general;
- Ensure that extensive publicity is given to the message against small arms, educate the media on the challenge posed by these weapons, especially the circulation of such weapons and the dynamic forces that cause and sustain armed conflicts;
- Secure the adoption of legislation in favour of disarmament and regulation of the circulation of firearms and bringing the discussion of arms and security issues to the people.

Local capacity-building

This relates basically to strengthening the ability of citizens to participate in political decision-making and entrenching a culture of peace. At this level, action by civil society involves such steps as:

- Training local community leaders in peace-building and conflict resolution techniques;
- Running awareness-building programmes so as to replace the culture of violence by a culture of peace;
- Organizing training seminars for senior customs, police and immigration officials on national and international rules governing the circulation of small arms;
- Educating communities about arms flows and the dynamic forces that encourage armed conflicts, and also helping the mass media to pass on the message to the larger public;
- Organizing seminars and training workshops on peaceful conflict resolution and peace-building for communities involved in armed conflicts;
- Educating communities on the virtues of participatory democracy and democratic leadership.

Demobilization, reorientation and reintegration

In societies emerging from armed conflict, civil-society organizations could help:

- To link small arms collection and monitoring programmes and measures to combat poverty and promote economic and social development;
- To develop innovative initiatives to build trust in the community;
- To supervise public destruction of collected stocks of weapons at the local level, under the control of all the stakeholders, in order to reassure communities that weapons taken out of circulation will not fall once again into the hands of criminals.

Role of surveillance and monitoring

The responsibilities of civil-society organizations in this field include:

- Monitoring contracts relating to arms purchases and reporting any abuses;
- Raising awareness and training the public in monitoring techniques of this type;
- Issuing constant reminders to the government that it should keep its promises relating to regulation of the circulation of small arms.

Research activities

Civil-society organizations are well positioned to explore ways in which research and public discussions can contribute to the development of local and regional policies for monitoring the proliferation of small arms. Civil-society organizations can, in particular:

- Initiate research projects aimed at awareness creation and information for the public concerning the nature and extent of the proliferation of small arms;
- Examine the factors that encourage the acquisition and possession of such weapons;
- Analyse the sources of small arms and the size of the stocks in circulation;
- Study arrangements and methods for the collection and marking of weapons.

Dissemination of information on small arms

Civil-society organizations can:

- Inform the public through information bulletins, magazines and electronic media about the proliferation of small arms and its consequences, as well as information on laws governing the acquisition and possession of firearms, the use of such weapons and penalties for unlawful possession or use;
- Advocate restrictions on the acquisition of weapons by individuals and strengthening of the capacity of the state to protect citizens;
- Provide information on the distinction between the lawful and unlawful acquisition, possession and use of firearms.

CONCLUSION

The necessary role of civil society in combating small arms is now widely acknowledged. In societies plagued by armed conflict, it is important to seek, above and beyond initiatives launched by the state, alternative ways and means of conflict resolution and peace-building. Civil society in West Africa has demonstrated that it can play a complementary role in states' efforts. But action by local communities and civil-society organizations can be effective only if it enjoys firm financial and human support from West African governments and the international community.

CHAPTER 13

THE ROLE OF THE MASS MEDIA IN STRENGTHENING A CULTURE OF PEACE AND NATIONAL INTEGRATION IN NIGERIA

Tonnie Iredia

INTRODUCTION

The mass media and national integration: a historical perspective

Iwe Irohin, the first newspaper in Nigeria, was founded in 1859. Its main purpose was to propagate the "virtues of Christianity". It did not question colonialism. Between 1859 and 1960, the indigenous press prepared Nigerians for independence and for political and economic leadership. Many researchers confirm that the media of the time were generally patriotic, competent and well informed; they helped to educate Nigerians about the evils in colonialism and the virtues of independence; the constituted a factor for unity and contributed to national integration. Not only did the media of the time contribute to uniting all Nigerians in the struggle against colonialism, but they also helped to extract concessions from the colonial authorities and criticized the excesses of the settlers and their local collaborators. Journalists forced the indigenous authorities at that time—such as the traditional authorities in northern Nigeria—to be accountable to their community for their actions and to adopt a less oppressive line. Nnamdi Azikiwe, Ernest Ikoli, Herbert Macaulay, Obafemi Awolowo, Anthony Enahoro, Ibrahim Imam, etc. may be cited as charismatic and patriotic media professionals of that time. In their work, they constantly emphasized the need to respect and take account of the opinion of the local people on the way they were governed by the settlers. In contrast to the *Nigerian Citizen* and the *Daily Times*, which were moderate because they were edited by Europeans at that time, the nationalist press was radical in its support of indigenous interests. It is, for instance, a fact that the Governor, Lord Lugard, maintained extremely difficult relations with the Nigerian press.

THE MASS MEDIA AS A THREAT TO NATIONAL INTEGRATION

Yet the mass media have not always been in harmony with the people. After independence, the role of the mass media has on occasion been harmful to national unity. Indeed, the prospect of independence badly shook the foundations of national peace and integration which had been laid when all Nigerians were united in the struggle against colonialism. As the politicians from the regions in northern Nigeria began to express apprehension concerning possible domination of the national political scene by their colleagues from the southern regions, what was known as the "pro-southern" press became increasingly impatient. It is possible that this "southern press" may have feared the possibility of a possible "conspiracy" against independence between the "pro-northern" elements and the colonial authorities. The North, on the other hand, did not at this time have its own media (newspapers or radio stations) to express its positions and "hit back". This situation motivated the "North" to establish the *New Nigerian Newspaper*, *Gaskiya Tafi Kabo* and Radio Television Kaduna. In this way, the seeds of mutual suspicion and discord were sown. Since then, the press has always played a significant role in dividing Nigerians along North/South and East/West lines, etc. Anifowose stated in 1982 that the regional elections of 1965 in the west of the country gave the Nigerian press an opportunity for war in which the media in the west and those in the east vied with each other in making comments which were equally insulting on both sides, along well-defined regional and ethnic lines. Indeed, many analysts believe that the psychological warfare which resulted from this situation undermined the national political system significantly and prepared the ground for the very first military coup in 1966.

CONSTITUTIONAL AND LEGISLATIVE PROVISIONS

Following this change of attitude on the part of the media, it was necessary to promote peace in Nigeria. This concern led decision makers to insert in various official documents provisions designed to define a culture of peace (National Constitution, Report of the Political Bureau, document on national mass communications policy, etc.). The 1987 report of the Political Bureau, for example, entrusted the mass media with such tasks as:

- Contributing to efforts to tackle underdevelopment, especially in rural areas;
- Contributing to efforts to combat tribalism, regionalism and corruption and promote responsible governance, so as to guarantee economic self-sufficiency and the fair distribution of wealth;
- Campaigning for the appointment of competent, devoted and honest individuals to posts of responsibility;
- Promoting the unity of the Nigerian nation and combating division, hatred, sectionalism and religious intolerance;
- Conducting civic education campaigns through the mass media and working to ensure respect for the rights and duties of citizens;
- Encouraging dialogue and the exchange of ideas;
- Creating socio-political conditions which would enable people to watch over their interests more effectively;
- Bridging the communication gap between town and country.

In support of these recommendations of the Political Bureau, the national mass communication policy emphasizes the need to promote "the positive aspects of our national values, our image, our unity and our stability", to campaign for national unity and integration, in particular by publishing objective and balanced analyses on issues of national interest. The press is also expected to promote a Nigerian national consciousness and the emergence of a just, humane and self-reliant society.

In the same vein, section 15 (i) of the 1999 Nigerian Constitution stipulates that national integration must be actively encouraged, while discrimination on the grounds of sex, religion, status or ethnic, linguistic or other association must be prohibited. Other fundamental principles designed to promote national integration lay down that that it is the duty of the Nigerian state to encourage the free movement of people and guarantee residence rights for citizens in all parts of the Federation.

In view of the current political and social reality in Nigeria, it is obvious that the objectives set forth are far from having been fully achieved.

MEDIA, PEACE AND NATIONAL INTEGRATION: SOCIOLOGICAL CONTEXT

The mass media in Nigeria today are made up of over 250 radio stations, around 100 newspapers and about 30 magazines.

If this impressive array of media power could be harnessed in the interests of national peace and integration, the atmosphere of hatred which threatens the very existence of the Nigerian nation, as well as its cultural values, would be rapidly neutralized. The media can be put to the service of the good cause. MacBride (*Many Voices, One World*, Ibadan: Ibadan University Press, 1981) states that "the media of communication are cultural instruments, which serve to promote or influence attitudes to motivate, to foster the spread of behaviour patterns and to bring about social integration". Regarding African media in particular, Mytton (*Mass Communication in Africa*, London: Edward Arnold Publishers, 1983) notes that "in some countries, they operate more as an extension of the media of the developed world, and consequently portray the ideas, values and culture of the rich societies. This seems to be especially true of the cinema and television. Few African cinemas even show feature films made locally ... Where television is concerned, the situation is scarcely different: Some African televisions purchase as much as 80 per cent of their material from European and United States sources".

The mass media can assist in building national unity by promoting national languages, for example. Until 1986, the national language problem had existed for a long time in a country like the Philippines, for example. Storey (*What is Cultural Studies*, London: Arnold Woddler Groups, 1996) explains how the solution was found by Filipinos: "(In Philippines) English was the language that seemed linguistically to unify a country inhabited by people who speak more than 70 regional languages and dialects ... In 1986, however, has seen the spectacular and spontaneous emergence of one of the native languages, Tagalog, as a popular national language ... it became an emblem of national self-esteem. Now, most television shows and newscasts in Tagalog are drawing far larger audiences than those in English".

This is a clear indication of what the mass media can do when they are supported in their efforts by a strong political will.

CULTURE OF PROFESSIONAL MEDIA AND CULTURE OF PEACE

Professional ethics

Reporting of political issues by the media is a good parameter that can be used to evaluate both the professional ethics and the role of journalists in fostering peace and national integration. Reports on social and political issues by the Nigerian media would benefit from greater depth. What is more, the integrity and competence of most journalists are not always guaranteed. In Nigeria, many people firmly believe it unthinkable that the radio, television or the newspapers could publish things which are not true, that is to day, lies. For the majority of Nigerians, any information published by the media is accepted as the "Gospel truth". This blind trust which the people place in the mass media can be effectively harnessed in the cause of peace and national unity. Unfortunately, the mass media do not appear to be working hard to guarantee their credibility; they do not seem to be aware of the great service they can perform for society. This lack of awareness of the challenges on the part of the media undoubtedly explains why any person can set himself or herself up as a "communication adviser" and tell even professional journalists how to behave, without shocking anyone. Such an attitude is quite simply unthinkable in other professions. Comparison between the journalist and the medical doctor is illustrative for this purpose. Both the journalist and the doctor are employed by rich businessmen who own newspapers and clinics. Whereas it would never occur to the owner of a clinic to tell the doctors working there how best to examine and treat patients, in the world of the media, the golden rule is still "he who pays the piper calls the tune". This is one of the reasons for the very poor level of ethics, objectivity and credibility that undermines the world of the media in Nigeria today.

Professional skills

The regional ownership of the media in Nigeria accounts for the lack of nationalism and the flourishing of anti-patriotism to be found in this milieu. What exists in Nigeria today are regional (and not national) media. In fact, one of the key tasks of the media in Nigeria is to reflect or publicize the views and sentiments of the regional elites who occupy important offices in the federal government or the National Assembly. This regrettable situation can be rectified by training media women and men who are creative and patriotic and can pay tribute to this constructive leadership that is expected from the media. In the past, Nigeria was fortunate in benefiting from the faith of such women and men, especially in the struggle against colonialism and the post-colonial military dictatorship. Today, the media are expected to denounce the abuse of power, from whatever source, and also to inform citizens of their rights and duties vis-à-vis the state. Only in this way can the media make an effective contribution to strengthening national peace and integration.

Pressure exerted on the media

Experience shows that the media are generally the target of controversy in sensitive political times: elections, campaigns against corruption or armed conflict. These are times when journalists are easily blackmailed; they are accused of being ill-intentioned, and sometimes they are simply killed. The perception of the Nigerian journalist by Nigerian citizens is deplorable. As emphasized by Bolaji Abdullahi ("The Fear of Freedom", *This Day*, Lagos, 1 November 2002), it is frightening that in Nigeria today, "a journalist is not just a journalist, he is [first and foremost] a 'Hausa journalist', an 'Ibo journalist', a 'Yoruba journalist', a Tiv, Niger Delta journalist etc.".

Yet the ethnic diversity of Nigeria on its own is not a source of tension. It cannot by itself threaten national peace and integration. The current crises are orchestrated by socio-economic factors, which are not seriously and objectively reported by the media. There is no doubt that a combination of factors resulting in particular from the regional loyalties of the media and the structure of power within the world of the media could offer a better explanation of the origin of the current problems. There is also the fear and irritation of certain media-poor regions of Nigeria at the overwhelming "media domination" of other regions. In 1999, for example, a large number of opinion leaders held a meeting on the subject of "Reporting the north: in search of an objective media". Such an initiative and the topic speak for themselves.

Relations between the government and the media

In general, the media professional who does his or her job objectively and courageously is rarely on good terms with the political world. We have mentioned that Lord Lugard nourished a deep hatred for the Nigerian press. Similarly, Napoleon Bonaparte declared that he would rather be faced by an enemy battalion than be criticized by the press. On the other hand, President Thomas Jefferson, the author of the United States Declaration of Independence and third President of the country, liked to say that were it left for him to decide whether to have a government without the press, or the press without government, he would not hesitate to choose the latter. A truly democratic government considers the media as a means of explaining its work to the public and a channel through which the political authorities are regularly informed of the wishes, reactions and aspirations of the people. There is no doubt that people who are better informed can make more effective contributions to the running of the country.

Peace-building through the mass media

The mass media can contribute to building national peace and unity. But in order to do so they must be supported by well-informed political leadership and civil society. For instance, in Nigeria, the National Orientation Agency, which is working for the enhancement of national integration through proactive strategies for conflict resolution, enjoys solid support both from the mass media and from local communities.

The media have tremendous power. This power can be potentially destructive or constructive, depending on what use is made of it. It is therefore important that, in the interests of peace and unity, the mass media should learn to work to eradicate mutual suspicion and hatred both between ethnic, religious and regional groups and between the political parties. To achieve this, media professionals need better working conditions and good professional skills. At present, for example, the material situation of Nigerian journalists leaves much to be desired. To ensure that the media make an effective contribution in the task of national peace-building and integration, the training of Nigerian journalists must be improved. In particular, courses on patriotism, nationalism, crisis management, conflict resolution, ethics, etc., should be included in the curricula of schools of journalism, in addition to upgrading of training facilities and infrastructure.

CONCLUSION

The mass media can be an effective tool for fostering national peace and integration. The challenge lies in the adoption by all of ethical and professional standards which will enable journalists to contribute to lessening social tensions and enhancing national unity. Media professionals need to provide information with objectivity, particularly on issues which affect or can endanger national peace and unity. Journalists should display more commitment and loyalty to the nation (as opposed to regional loyalties which threaten national unity). Another factor to consider is the use of English by the media, in a country where the vast majority of citizens can neither read nor write English. In other words, it is important to pay attention to both the form and the substance of the media message: the language used by the media should be accessible to the people, especially as the content of the message, relating to peace, concerns them all.

RECENT UNIDIR PUBLICATIONS[1]

| Research Reports / Rapports de recherche |

Multilateral Diplomacy and the NPT: An Insider's Account, by Jayantha Dhanapala with Randy Rydell, in cooperation with SIPRI, 2005, 206p., United Nations publication, Sales No. GV.E.05.0.5.

Peace in the Middle East: P2P and the Israeli-Palestinian Conflict, by Adel Atieh, Gilad Ben-Nun, Gasser El Shahed, Rana Taha and Steve Tulliu, 2004, 54p., United Nations publication, Sales No. GV.E.05.0.2.

Building a Weapons of Mass Destruction Free Zone in the Middle East: Global Non-Proliferation Regimes and Regional Experiences, in cooperation with the League of Arab States, 2004, 310p., United Nations publication, Sales No. GV.E.04.0.30.

Implementing the United Nations Programme of Action on Small Arms and Light Weapons: Analysis of the Reports Submitted by States in 2003, by Elli Kytömäki and Valerie Anne Yankey-Wayne, in cooperation with UNDP, DDA and SAS, 2004, 320p., United Nations publication, Sales No. GV.E.04.0.27.

Open Skies: A Cooperative Approach to Military Transparency and Confidence Building, by Pál Dunay, Márton Krasznai, Hartwig Spitzer, Rafael Wiemker and William Wynne, 2004, 340p., United Nations publication, Sales No. GV.E.04.0.18.

A Guide to the Destruction of Small Arms and Light Weapons—The Approach of the South African National Defence Force, by Sarah Meek and Noel Stott, in cooperation with SAS, 2004, 76p., United Nations publication, Sales No. GV.E.04.0.5.

Costs of Disarmament—Mortgaging the Future: The South Asian Arms Dynamic, by Susan Willett, 2004, 124p., United Nations publication, Sales No. GV.E.04.0.1.

---

[1] For a complete list, please see our Web site at http://www.unidir.org, or contact Anita Blétry: Tel.: +41(0)22 917 42 63, Fax: +41 (0)22 917 01 76, abletry@unog.ch.

After Non-Detection, What?—What Iraq's Unfound WMD Mean for the Future of Non-Proliferation, by Michael Friend, 2003, 32p., United Nations publication, UNIDIR/2003/38.

Outer Space and Global Security, in cooperation with Ploughshares and Simons Centre for Peace and Disarmament Studies, 2003, 104p., United Nations publication, Sales No. GV.E.03.0.26.

Costs of Disarmament—Disarming the Costs: Nuclear Arms Control and Nuclear Rearmament, by Susan Willett, 2003, 174p., United Nations publication, Sales No. GV.E.03.0.25.

Desarme nuclear: Regímenes internacional, latinoaméricano y argentino de no proliferación, por Marcelo F. Valle Fonrouge, 2003, 146p., United Nations publication, Sales No. GV.S.03.0.24.

Coming to Terms with Security: A Lexicon for Arms Control, Disarmament and Confidence-Building, by Steve Tulliu and Thomas Schmalberger, 2003, 252p., United Nations publication, Sales No. GV.E/A.03.0.21.
* Also available in Arabic, 278p., Sales No. GV.E/A.03.0.21.
* Also available in Spanish, 548p., Sales No. GV.E/S.03.0.29.
* Also available in Korean, 626p., UNIDIR/2003/30.

Destroying Surplus Weapons: An Assessment of Experience in South Africa and Lesotho, by Sarah Meek and Noel Stott, in coooperation with SAS, 2003, 102p., United Nations publication, Sales No. GV.E.03.0.18.

Lutte contre la prolifération des armes légPres en Afrique de l'Ouest: Manuel de formation des forces armées et de sécurité, sous la direction de Anatole Ayissi et Ibrahima Sall, en coopération avec le PCASED et la CEDEAO, 2003, 150p., publication des Nations Unies, numéro de vente: GV.F.03.0.17.

Coming to Terms with Security: A Handbook on Verification and Compliance, in cooperation with VERTIC, 2003, 158p., United Nations publication, Sales No. GV.E/A.03.0.12.
* Also available in Arabic, 172p., Sales No. GV.E/A.03.0.12.

Internal Conflict and Regional Security in South Asia: Approaches, Perspectives and Policies, by Shiva Hari Dahal, Haris Gazdar, S.I. Keethaponcalan and Padmaja Murthy, 2003, 62p., United Nations publication, Sales No. GV.E.03.0.10.

The Scope and Implications of a Tracing Mechanism for Small Arms and Light Weapons, in cooperation with SAS, 2003, 238p., United Nations publication, Sales No. GV.E.03.0.7.

* Existe également en français: ***Portée et implications d'un mécanisme de traçage des armes légères et de petit calibre***, en coopération avec SAS, 2003, 264p., publication des Nations Unies, numéro de vente: GV.F.03.0.07.

Participatory Monitoring of Humanitarian Mine Action: Giving Voice to Citizens of Nicaragua, Mozambique and Cambodia, by Susan Willett (ed.), 2003, 122p., United Nations publication, Sales No. GV.E.03.0.6.

The Treaty of Pelindaba on the African Nuclear-Weapon-Free Zone, by Oluyemi Adeniji, 2002, 332p., United Nations publication, Sales No. GV.E.03.0.5.

Project Coast: Apartheid's Chemical and Biological Warfare Programme, by Chandré Gould and Peter Folb, in cooperation with the Centre for Conflict Resolution, 2002, 300p., United Nations publication, Sales No. GV.E.02.0.10.

Tactical Nuclear Weapons: Time for Control, by Taina Susiluoto, 2002, 162p., United Nations publication, Sales No. GV.E.02.0.7.

Le Conseil de sécurité à l'aube du XXIème siècle : quelle volonté et quelle capacité a-t-il de maintenir la paix et la sécurité internationales ?, par Pascal Teixeira, en coopération avec l'IFRI, 2002, 106p., publication des Nations Unies, numéro de vente: GV.F.02.0.6.

* Also available in English: ***The Security Council at the Dawn of the Twenty-First Century: To What Extent Is It Willing and Able to Maintain International Peace and Security?***, by Pascal Teixeira, in cooperation with IFRI, 2003, 135p., United Nations publication, Sales No. GV.E.02.0.6.

Costs of Disarmament—Rethinking the Price Tag: A Methodological Inquiry into the Cost and Benefits of Arms Control, by Susan Willett, 2002, 70p., United Nations publication, Sales No. GV.E.02.0.3.

Missile Defence, Deterrence and Arms Control: Contradictory Aims or Compatible Goals?, in cooperation with Wilton Park, 2002, 39p., United Nations publication, UNIDIR/2002/4.

Disarmament as Humanitarian Action—A discussion on the occasion of the 20th anniversary of the United Nations Institute for Disarmament Research (UNIDIR), in cooperation with the United Nations Department for Disarmament Affairs (DDA), 2001, 24p., United Nations publication, UNIDIR/2001/23.

* Existe également en français: *Le désarmement comme action humanitaire*, en coopération avec le Département des affaires de désarmement de l'Organisation des Nations Unies, 2003, 30p., United Nations publication, UNIDIR/2003/7.

Cooperating for Peace in West Africa: An Agenda for the 21st Century, by Anatole Ayissi (ed.), 2001, 159p., United Nations publication, Sales No. GV.E/F.01.0.19 / *Coopération pour la paix en Afrique de l'Ouest : Agenda pour le XXIème siècle*, sous la direction d'Anatole Ayissi, 2001, 169p., publication des Nations Unies, numéro de vente : GV.E/F.01.0.19.

Illicit Trafficking in Firearms: Prevention and Combat in Rio de Janeiro, Brazil—A National, Regional and Global Issue, by Péricles Gasparini Alves, 2000, 66p., United Nations publication, Sales No. GV.E.01.0.2.

Tactical Nuclear Weapons: A Perspective from Ukraine, by A. Shevtsov, A. Yizhak, A. Gavrish and A. Chumakov, 2001, 95p., United Nations publication, Sales No. GV.E.01.0.1.

Tactical Nuclear Weapons: Options for Control, by William C. Potter, Nikolai Sokov, Harald Müller and Annette Schaper, 2000, 87p., United Nations publication, Sales No. GV.E.00.0.21.

Bound to Cooperate: Conflict, Peace and People in Sierra Leone, by Anatole Ayissi and Robin-Edward Poulton (eds), 2000, 213p., United Nations publication, Sales No. GV.E.00.0.20.

Coming to Terms with Security: A Lexicon for Arms Control, Disarmament and Confidence-Building, by Steve Tulliu and Thomas Schmalberger, 2000, 246p., United Nations publication, Sales No. GV.E.00.0.12.

The Small Arms Problem in Central Asia: Features and Implications, by Bobi Pirseyedi, 2000, 120p., United Nations publication, Sales No. GV.E.00.0.6.

Peacekeeping in Africa: Capabilities and Culpabilities, by Eric G. Berman and Katie E. Sams, 2000, 540p., United Nations publication, Sales No. GV.E.00.0.4.

West Africa Small Arms Moratorium: High-Level Consultations on the Modalities for the Implementation of PCASED, by Jacqueline Seck, 2000, 81p., United Nations publication, UNIDIR/2000/2 / *Moratoire ouest-africain sur les armes légères : Consultations de haut niveau sur les modalités de la mise en œuvre du PCASED*, par Jacqueline Seck, 2000, 83p., United Nations publication, UNIDIR/2000/2.

Disarmament Forum / *Forum du désarmement*
(quarterly / trimestriel)